By combining traditional treatment with novel behavioral exercises, Kill the Craving *offers addicts an interesting and unique approach to managing or elimating their cravings. ERP has created a new pathway in the treatment of addictions. It is one that offers hope and encouragement for both addicts and professionals.*

—Dr. Benjamin Primm
CEO and Founder, Addiction Research and
Treatment Corporation, New York, NY

Kill the Craving *offers a new behavioral treatment that can actually reduce the desire to abuse substances. This book will help patients successfully learn to resist cravings: something that is crucial to the recovery of every addicted patient. I recommend this book to patients and professionals alike. They will not be disappointed.*

—J Lincoln Duffy, M.D., Medical Director,
Putnam Hospital Center, Carmel, New York

Kill the Craving *is a truly useful approach to building a life of sobriety. It is realistic without being full of war stories and functions as a unique adjunctive tool to 12-step programs. Compatible for addictions of all types, and for the many varieties of people seeking recovery—be they adults, adolescents, dual diagnosed patients, individuals or groups—*Kill the Craving *is a refreshing addition to the literature on addictions and recovery.*

—Susanna Feder, Ph.D., Staff Psychologist,
Sarah Lawrence College, Bronxville, New York

KILL
THE CRAVING

HOW TO CONTROL THE IMPULSE
TO USE DRUGS AND ALCOHOL

JOSEPH SANTORO, PH.D., B.C.E.T.S.
ROBERT DELETIS, C.A.D.C.
ALFRED BERGMAN, M.S.

NEW HARBINGER PUBLICATIONS, INC.

Distributed in the U.S.A. by Publishers Group West; in Canada by Raincoast Books; in Great Britain by Airlift Book Company, Ltd.; in South Africa by Real Books, Ltd.; in Australia by Boobook; and in New Zealand by Tandem Press.

Copyright © 2001 by Joseph Santoro, Robert DeLetis, and Alfred Bergman
      New Harbinger Publications, Inc.
      5674 Shattuck Avenue
      Oakland, CA 94609

Cover design by Lightbourne Images
Illustrations by Thomas Mortimer
Edited by Jason Rath
Text design by Michele Waters

ISBN 1-57224-237-X Paperback

New Harbinger Publications' Web site address: www.newharbinger.com

03   02   01

10   9   8   7   6   5   4   3   2   1

First printing

*To my son, Zeke, who continues to amaze me, inspire me,
and most of all, allow me to grow more each day. I love you.*

RJD

*To my wife, Jeanne, and daughter, Nicole, who provided me
with the time and quiet needed to complete this book.*

JS

*To Betsy, Heather, and Aaron thank you for
your enduring love and support.*

AB

Contents

Preface

Here are two simple questions.

1. Are you addicted?

2. Do you want to do something about it?

This book can help to free you from your addictive cravings. It could even help to transform your life into one you no longer hate. Read this book. Surrender to the truth. And save your life.

It's that simple. Don't deny it, don't fight it—just let it happen.

—*The Authors*

A Note to Substance Abuse Treatment Professionals

Exposure Response Prevention or ERP can be used with your drug and alcohol addicted clients. In addition to the photo card format you can also desensitize your clients conditioned and cognitively mediated cravings through the use of simulated substances and the equipment used to prepare and use these substances. You can obtain a complete professional ERP kit for this purpose and inquire about training in ERP therapy by contacting any of the authors at 1-888-8-CARE-4U. You can also learn more about our ERP Professional Kit on our Web site at *www.killthecraving.com*. Your clients can also perform guided photo card ERP at this site as well. Online ERP is a helpful adjunct to office ERP therapy and generic substance abuse counseling.

Our Web site at *www.killthecraving.com* presents data on the effectiveness of this treatment method for clients with substance abuse problems. We found that in a study (Santoro, DeLitis, and McNamara) of 54 residential patients (of which 33 were treated with ERP and 24 were not) that the ERP treated group of patients were less likely to relapse (55 percent versus 88 percent) and were more likely to report being abstinent at the time of follow-up (91 percent versus 42 percent). Both results were statistically significant at the .02 levels or better. The full text of our study can be downloaded at the site.

ERP has the potential to become a new and valuable therapeutic tool to treat people with serious substance abuse problems. We welcome your feedback and commentary.

Acknowledgments

The authors would like to thank the following people for their invaluable help in researching and developing the ERP therapy protocol. Our thanks go out to Maggie McNamara, and Mike Katsarakes. Maggie was especially helpful in analyzing the efficacy of ERP therapy.

A special thanks goes to our families, who endured the loss of many hours of family time that would have been theirs had we not devoted it to writing this book.

Introduction

Kill the Craving introduces a new tool for the treatment of drug and alcohol addictions. This tool addresses the core problem every recovering addict faces—the need to reduce his craving to use drugs and alcohol (Baker et al. 1987). *Kill the Craving* teaches the recovering addict how to apply exposure response prevention (ERP) technology to this task. ERP is a behavior therapy treatment technique (Drummond et al. 1995). It has been successfully used for over two decades to treat obsessive-compulsive disorders and phobias. ERP is not a magic bullet. It is not a substitute for an affirmative decision to fight off your addiction. It is not a substitute for a community support group. But it is a new tool that you can use to help win the addiction war.

This book presents a self-administered form of ERP called photo card ERP. To help the addict prepare for doing ERP, the book helps him explore his motivation for using drugs and alcohol and his readiness to modify his use patterns. We then discuss deep-breathing relaxation and body-tension scanning before introducing the self-administered form of ERP and how to apply it to addictive cravings for cocaine, crack, alcohol, marijuana, or heroin. The book closes with chapters on lifestyle repair and relapse prevention.

Throughout the book you are urged to focus on what you are gaining—not giving up—by getting and staying clean and sober. Stories about real patients help to illustrate key points.

For many people addiction is a passion. It fills a void deep in the soul that defies easy description. One addict wrote of his passion with these words:

> *Eventually I found my love. My first love was with alcohol. My first drink was the start of a long but dysfunctional relationship. My parents drank and they were in love as well. I craved and desired love from my parents but they were unable to express their feelings. Don't get me wrong, they cared for me but they did not nurture me in the way I needed. But alcohol filled that void very well. That first drink was spectacular. I loved it! It made me feel warm and comfortable inside. It gave me unconditional love and accepted me without making any demands on me.*

Breaking away from so passionate a relationship is no easy feat. The obsession to use can be all-powerful, and few outsiders can understand just how hypnotic it is. Loved ones, career, money, and even life itself will be used and abused to meet its compulsive demands. Woe to those who come between an addict and her addiction, for they will be trampled upon. The addict does not hate those whom she uses (she may even love them). She is simply caught up in the momentum of her obsession with an ongoing, death-defying high.

If you are an addict, you need to think about what your addiction is doing to you and your lifestyle. If you are the loved one or friend of an addict, you need to understand how powerful, dangerous, and out-of-control an addiction really is and what you can do to help. This book can help both of you. It provides a way to understand the motivational dynamics of addiction. It provides a structured method for overcoming the compulsion to use addictive substances. It provides hope for a better future.

The first step for anyone using the techniques in this book—a step you should take before you even begin chapter 1—is to measure the intensity of your addiction. The Addiction Intensity Scale (AIS) on the following pages can help.

One of the first questions addicts need to ask themselves is, "How addicted am I?" The Addiction Intensity Scale (AIS) can help you answer this question. To use this scale check off all of the items that characterize your addiction. Be truthful.

Addiction Intensity Scale

Addiction Intensity Level	My Score	Criteria
Moderate Addiction	___/5 (3+)	▫ Using more than 5 times per week ▫ Able to work and pay bills ▫ Able to stop all use without help for at least 30 consecutive days ▫ Loved ones questioning whether you are getting addicted ▫ Spending more than $100 per week on addiction
Severe Addiction	___/10 (5+)	▫ Daily use is the rule ▫ "Crashes," blackouts, withdrawal symptoms occur ▫ Difficulty working, fired from jobs ▫ Using more than one substance (e.g., pot and alcohol) ▫ Lying to loved ones and friends about use ▫ Loved ones urging you to get treatment ▫ Some stealing from loved ones only to support addiction ▫ Cannot stop all use *without help* for longer than two weeks ▫ Suspended or revoked driver's license ▫ Arrested for possession or driving while impaired
Catastrophic Addiction	___/11 (6+)	▫ Daily heavy use ▫ Cannot work to support self ▫ Stealing from loved ones ▫ Fighting with loved ones about use ▫ Stealing from strangers at least once ▫ Owes money to dealers ▫ Weight loss, liver problems, or frequent sickness ▫ Cannot stop all use *without help* for longer than four days ▫ Spent up to 30 days in jail because of addiction ▫ Suspended or revoked professional license ▫ Family and friends are forcing you to get help

Terminal Addiction	___/10 (5+)	□ Daily heavy use, near continuous use □ Cannot stop all use *without help* for more than 24 hours □ Homeless or near homeless □ Regular stealing to support addiction □ Physical health problems are getting worse □ Spent more than 30 days in jail because of addiction □ Have not been able to work at all □ On probation for addiction-related offenses □ You feel totally hopeless and unable to stop despite misery □ Friends and family have given up hope

In each section, give yourself one point for each item checked and write the total in the blank provided. If your score for each section is equal to or greater than the score in the parentheses below the score you write, you meet the criteria for that level of addiction. The highest level for which you meet the criteria is your overall addiction intensity score (AIS).

If you or someone you know meets the criteria for being at least moderately addicted, then this book can be a great help. If you are catastrophically or terminally addicted then you will also need intensive outpatient and residential help. **Do not attempt ERP on your own if your AIS score is that high.**

The first chapter will help you get the process of self-reflection and exploration started. If you have any questions about any of the information contained in this book you can call the authors at 1-888-8-CARE-4U or visit us on the Web at *www.killthecraving.com*. We will do our best to be helpful.

1

Hollow Voices and Elusive Highs

The Pleasure Wheel Spins

Why are addictive activities so attractive? Some people get off on drugs. Others do it with booze. Others bet it all. Still others get it through sexsexsexsexsex. Some gorge or starve themselves into shape. Some cut or burn themselves. And eventually every one plays cat and mouse with the Grim Reaper.

Whatever your addiction is, it is what it is because you just can't seem to get enough. Do you remember how it all got started? That first time, when you were a virgin. How did it feel? And what about those really great times? Do you remember them? You never thought you could get off like that. Remember how drunk you got . . . how the coke really electrified you . . . the heroin chilled you . . . that orgasm rocketed you? How you came so close to winning it really big? How great all that food felt going down . . . and how thin you were just *starting* to get? Do you remember? How long has it been since your "high" made you feel that good?

The good times, the high times, where are they now? Things have changed. It doesn't feel as good anymore. You've tried to find the buzz you used to get—and it's nowhere to be found. Maybe this is starting to scare you. Your (real) friends and your family, they're looking angry, hopeless, frustrated, and sad. Are they about ready to give up on you? Enablers are getting scarce. Reality (and maybe the law) is closing in. And you just don't know what to do. Or do you?

The Incredible Shrinking Lifestyle

You can take care of yourself. You know how to play the game. You can control your high. No way does it control you. It is not an addiction, and fuck you for saying it is. No one is going to tell you what to do.

Maybe you are having a tough time paying your bills. Maybe you've lost a lot of the energy you had. Maybe you are not sure of where you are going to be living. Maybe you are feeling really sick inside. Maybe someone you cared about died. Maybe—no, that will never happen!

You are smart. You know how to manipulate them. It's almost too easy. So what if they're giving up on you? So what if they're starting to pull away? You'll find more helpers. You always have.

So what'll it be? So what if your lifestyle is shrinking and you're alone. You can still use your high to make it all go away. Right?

No One Is an Island

But do you want to cut yourself off from your real friends and family? Your spouse, your lover, your parents, your kids, your best buddies, your sister, your brother, everyone you once loved and cared about? Can you remember how that felt? Or are you just numb?

What about the rest of your reality? Where you work, learn, play, eat, and wake up? What kind of shape is your lifestyle in? Do you have money in the bank? A warm bed? A car? A license? Can you look your friends in the eye? Can you go to a mirror, look at yourself, and say, "I love you"? Does anyone still love you? Do you care? Or are you an island surrounded by an addictive sea? Can you survive all alone? You can always get your high. Sure you can . . . so fuck them all.

Comfortably Numb

Roger is a young man in his mid-twenties. He works as a bar manager and parties hard several times a week. A couple of dozen shots and lines of cocaine are on his party menu from 9 P.M. to 4 A.M. as often as seven days a week. One night Roger was heading home in his car at a leisurely 140 miles per hour. His head was buzzed into a blur. He misjudged a turn and slammed his car into an embankment. Miraculously, he only dislocated his shoulder and badly bruised his face when his air bag deployed. His car was totaled and he was arrested. Luckily, Roger's brother had connections with the police and he was able to get the charges reduced and help Roger avoid jail time. Roger vowed that he would stop his partying. This resolution dissolved once his injuries healed. Roger went back to his alcohol and drugs.

Lately he started to worry about the blackouts he has been experiencing. The other day he noticed that he had injured himself above his eye, but he could not recall how it happened. His friends told him later that when he had passed out the night before, the corner of his eye caught a piece of concrete curb. Roger felt a little worried. He also was starting to get concerned about the fact that he had lost about twenty pounds and hadn't eaten anything for the last six days. People tell him that he doesn't look too good. Roger isn't sure whether all his partying is good for him anymore. He is looking for an easy solution, but he is so numb that he barely cares.

Thinking About Change

Does Roger's experience remind you of what you are going through now? Do you still think that you can drug and drink but avoid becoming addicted? Are you feeling so "comfortably numb" that you hardly care what's happening to you? Are your friends and family getting scared and frustrated with you?

Even if your life is beginning to feel out of control you can always make the choice to stop and take a long clear look at what you are really doing to yourself. For many addicts, making this first decision, taking the first step, is frightening. Giving up an addictive substance—especially all at once—can be too daunting to even consider. But overcoming an addiction isn't an all-or-nothing event. Some people cut back first, reducing the most dangerous parts of their addiction before tackling the rest of it. Twelve-step programs preach that it has to be all or nothing, but that approach doesn't work for everyone. We believe that a small start is better than no start. *Kill the Craving* offers you a different starting point for becoming un-addicted. Instead of asking you to suddenly begin avoiding everything associated with your addiction, it asks you to directly confront the objects of your addiction in order to *overcome* you impulse to use, rather than simply resist or ignore the impulse. This differs from the twelve-step approach's advice to avoid people, places, and things associated with addiction.

Are you feeling comfortably numb or out of control?

Controlling the Impulse

People who are addicted think they're in control. People who run rehab programs tell them they aren't. When the addict insists, the rehab people say he is in denial. The rehab people confront the addict until he admits that he is out of control. Once the addict surrenders the belief that he is in control, he can work the rehab program. Once he admits that he is helpless, he can accept help, get free, and stay free.

But how can someone who isn't in control of his or her addiction decisions get free of addictive behavior? Is it the program, the support group, or the addict's higher power that makes this possible? A little known fact: Majorities of people who get addicted to something (drugs, cigarettes, alcohol) stop their addictions without a rehab program or formal support group. How do these people manage this feat if they are not in control of their addictive behaviors?

Being in control of something means that you make decisions about it. Sometimes your decisions produce the results you want. Sometimes they don't. You have equal control of your good and bad decisions. When you make a bad decision, the cause can often be traced to a lack of knowledge, experience, forward planning, anticipation, or skill. Sometimes your values (or lack thereof) lead you to a bad choice, but you never make good or bad decisions because you are not in control. Making decisions means control. So what are those rehab programs referring to when they say, "You are out of control?" We believe that they confuse a pattern of *bad* decision-making (such as the pattern of substance abuse) with not being in control of the *act* of decision-making. When they say you are in denial, what they really mean is that you are ignoring the negative consequences that your decisions produce. But you are still in control of your decisions, even though you may be "blind" to their full effects.

If you want to start to think about controlling your addictive impulses, you begin by thinking about the results that they have produced lately. Then you decide whether the results please you. If they do, then you continue your addiction. If they don't, you need to weaken your desire to use and develop a plan for reducing your addictive activity to a pleasing and healthy level.

But how do you evaluate whether your recent decisions please you? And if part of an addiction's nature is to "blind" you to negative consequences, how can you even be sure you are *seeing* all the results? The next sections of this self-help guide are for those who are ready to evaluate the results of their addictive decisions and the satisfaction they produce.

2

My Lifestyle's Balance Sheet

Everyone should periodically evaluate her lifestyle's balance sheet to determine her Net Lifestyle Satisfaction (NLS). Your lifestyle is composed of everything you do. It is a collection of all the activities and places that define who you are as a person. Your lifestyle has a strong emotional impact on you. If your lifestyle's net effect leaves you feeling bad about yourself then changes in it are needed. If your lifestyle leaves you feeling good, then all is right in the world. Your task in this chapter is to discover how your lifestyle makes you feel. Evaluating your lifestyle is a lot like doing some spring cleaning. Things need to be sorted out. What you want is kept and what you no longer want is discarded. Here's a step-by-step plan that will help you do this.

Your lifestyle is composed of several major parts: work, family, friends, intimate relationships, recreational activities (and energy boosters), self-development, money, future plans, spiritual connections, and values.

To evaluate each part of your lifestyle we've developed a system of worksheets that will walk you through the evaluation process. Each worksheet will determine:

1. What is included in that part of your lifestyle.

2. How much true satisfaction you get from your lifestyle.

3. How important your lifestyle is to you.

4. What it costs you to develop and maintain it.

5. What you would like to change about it if anything.

6. How important making such changes is to you right now.

You will use a separate worksheet (you may photocopy them) to evaluate each part of your lifestyle. You will need a calculator to do the math. You can also use our Web site to do your lifestyle analysis. Your password is the last five digits of the ISBN book number found at the beginning of the book on the copyright page. Your user name is "bookreader." If you don't understand something, ask your counselor or contact us by phone at 1-888-8-CARE-4U or on the Web at *www.killthecraving.com*.

The first worksheet will help you evaluate the work part of your lifestyle.

Work

Use the worksheet on page 17 as you consider the following questions about work. What type of work do you do? How did you choose your current employer? Do you enjoy your work for itself or is it just a paycheck? Do you like your boss? Do you like the people you work with? Do you see yourself working in the same job and organization five years from now? Write your thoughts in section A of the worksheet.

Given your answers to the above questions, how satisfied are you with your work? Use a 0 to 100 scale to rate your satisfaction. A rating of 100 means, "I am totally satisfied; it's the best thing in my life." A zero means, "I absolutely hate it all the time." Place your rating in the space provided in section B of the worksheet.

How important is your work to your lifestyle? Could you cut it out of your life today and not need or miss it? Rate its importance on the same 0 to 100 scale. Place your rating in the space provided in section C on the worksheet.

How much psychological and physical energy does your work demand of you? How much stress does it generate? How exhausted do you feel at the end of your workweek? Again use a 0 to 100 scale, but this time you need to rate the percentage of your total psychophysical energy that your work consumes each week. To figure this out, consider how much energy it consumes in relation to the other parts of your life. The total of all the energy ratings for the nine parts of your lifestyle cannot exceed 100, so keep track of how much of the 100 energy units you have left to use as you move from worksheet to worksheet. Place your rating in the space provided in section D on the worksheet.

Now you're ready to list what, if anything, you would like to change about your work. Do you want to change employer, position, or get a promotion? Be as specific as you can. If you know you want to make some kind of change but cannot specify it, put that down. This could be important later. How important are making these changes (or specifying what they are) to you? Use the 0 to 100 scale, where 100 equals "critically important, my lifestyle depends upon it," to 0 equals "no importance at all." Record your answer in section E.

When you have finished the worksheet, write your "work net" number on the Work Net line of the form on page 17.

Net Lifestyle Satisfaction Worksheet

Date:

PART: MY WORK

A. Define your work:

B. Rate your work satisfaction: (0 = none; 100 = high)

C. Rate the importance of your work: (0 = none; 100 = high)

D. Percentage of psychophysical energy consumed by work: (0 to 100%)

Changes you would like to make in your work:

□ none

□ uncertain

E. Rate the importance of these changes/uncertainty: (0 = none; 100 = high)

WORK Summary

(_____ + _____) x _____ = _____
 Satisfaction rating   Importance rating   Energy percentage   WORK NET
 (Section B score)   (Section C score)   (Section D score)

CHANGES

□ none

□ yes

□ uncertain

Importance Rating _____
   (Section E)

Family

Use the worksheet on page 19 to answer these questions.

Who do you consider to be a part of your family? Include biological and psychological members. Exclude those with whom you do not share a positive emotional bond. This will require you to do some honest thinking. Write your answers in section A of the worksheet.

How much true satisfaction do you get from your family as defined above? Rate it on 0 to 100 scale where 100 equals "amazing satisfaction" and 0 equals "none." Record your rating in section B.

How important is your defined family to you? Use a similar 0 to 100 scale, and record you answer in section C.

What is the psychophysical energy cost of maintaining and enhancing your relationships with your family? Remember to use a piece of a 100-point pie. Your total for all of your lifestyle parts cannot exceed 100. Write your response in section D.

What changes, if any, would you like to make in your family? If you're uncertain say so. How important are making these changes to you at this time in your life? Use the 0 to 100 scale where 0 equals "no importance" and 100 equals "critical to my lifestyle." Record your response in section E.

When you have completed the worksheet, write your "family net" number on the Family Net line of the form on page 19.

Net Lifestyle Satisfaction Worksheet

Date:
PART: MY FAMILY
A. Define your family:
B. Rate your family satisfaction: (0 = none; 100 = high)
C. Rate the importance of your family: (0 = none; 100 = high)
D. Percentage of your energy consumed by your family: (0 to 100%)
Changes you would like to make in your family: □ none □ uncertain
E. Rate the importance of these changes/uncertainty: (0 = none; 100 = high)

FAMILY Summary

(_____ + _____) x _____ = _____

Satisfaction rating   Importance rating   Energy percentage   FAMILY NET
(Section B score)   (Section C score)   (Section D score)

CHANGES

□ none

□ yes

□ uncertain

Importance Rating _____
  (Section E)

Friends

Use the worksheet on page 21 as you consider the following questions. Record you answers in the appropriate spaces on the worksheet. Whom do you consider to be a part of your circle of friends? Exclude business-only friends and casual acquaintances. Name all of your true friends.

How much true satisfaction do you get from your friends as defined above? Rate it on a 0 to 100 scale where 100 equals "amazing satisfaction" and 0 equals "none."

How important is your defined circle of friends to you? Use a similar 0 to 100 scale.

What is the psychophysical energy cost of maintaining and enhancing your relationships with your friends? Remember to take a percentage of a 100-point pie. Your total for all of your lifestyle parts cannot exceed 100.

What changes, if any, would you like to make in your friends? Do you want to find new friends? Do you want to end some relationships? If you're uncertain say so. How important is making these changes to you at this time in your life? Use the 0 to 100 scale where 100 equals "critical to my lifestyle" and 0 equals "no importance."

When you have completed the worksheet, write your "friends net" number on the Friends Net line of the form on page 21.

Net Lifestyle Satisfaction Worksheet

Date:
PART: MY FRIENDS
A. Define your friends:
B. Rate your friend satisfaction: (0 = none; 100 = high)
C. Rate the importance of your friends: (0 = none; 100 = high)
D. Percentage of your energy consumed by your friends: (0 to 100%)
Changes you would like to make in your friends: ☐ none ☐ uncertain
E. Rate the importance of these changes/uncertainty: (0 = none; 100 = high)

FRIENDS Summary

(_____ + _____) x _____ = _____

  Satisfaction rating   Importance rating   Energy percentage   FRIENDS NET
  (Section B score)   (Section C score)   (Section D score)

CHANGES

☐ none

☐ yes

☐ uncertain

Importance Rating _____
  (Section E)

Intimate Relationships or "Intimates"

This is a subcategory of friends and family. An intimate relationship is one in which there is a high level of trust, information sharing, and honesty. It may include physical and psychological intimacy or only psychological intimacy. It cannot be based only upon physical intimacy. Lovers, spouses, best friends, soul mates are all potential intimates. You do not have to share everything about yourself with someone for them to be an intimate, but there needs to be a valued bond of trust between you.

Use the worksheet on page 23 as you consider the following questions. Record your answers in the appropriate spaces on the worksheet. Whom do you consider to be your intimates? Make sure they meet the above definition.

How much true satisfaction do you get from your intimates as defined above? Rate it on a 0 to 100 scale where 100 equals "amazing satisfaction" and 0 equals "none."

How important are your intimates to you? Use the 0 to 100 scale.

What is the psychophysical energy cost of maintaining and enhancing your relationships with your intimates? Remember to take a percentage of a 100-point pie. Your total for all of your lifestyle parts cannot exceed 100.

What changes, if any, would you like to make in your intimates? Do you want to find additional intimates? Do you want to end some relationships? Do you want to deepen some relationships? If you're uncertain say so. How important are making these changes to you at this time in your life? Use the 0 to 100 scale for your rating.

When you have completed the worksheet, write your "intimates net" number on the Intimates Net line of the form on page 23.

Net Lifestyle Satisfaction Worksheet

Date:
PART: MY INTIMATES
A. Define your intimates:
B. Rate your intimates satisfaction: (0 = none; 100 = high)
C. Rate the importance of your intimates: (0 = none; 100 = high)
D. Percentage of your energy consumed by your intimates: (0 to 100%)
Changes you would like to make in your intimates: ☐ none ☐ uncertain
E. Rate the importance of these changes/uncertainty: (0 = none; 100 = high)

INTIMATES Summary

(_____ + _____) x _____ = _____
Satisfaction rating Importance rating   Energy percentage   INTIMATES NET
(Section B score)   (Section C score)   (Section D score)

CHANGES

☐ none

☐ yes

☐ uncertain

Importance Rating _____
   (Section E)

Recreation

Use the worksheet on page 25 as you consider the following questions. Record your answers in the appropriate space on the worksheet. What are your recreational activities, if any? List all that you do at least four times per year. A recreational activity should allow you to release stress, enjoy something different, or free your mind of everyday matters. It can be done alone or with others. They can include exercise, sports, hobbies, dieting, meditation, collecting, and so forth. And do not forget to include your addictive activities.

Rate your total satisfaction with all of the recreational activities that you have defined above. Use the 0 to 100 scale.

How important are your recreational activities? Use the 0 to 100 scale where 0 equals "no value to my life" and 100 equals "I cannot do without them." If you do not have any recreational activities then you rate this area an automatic 0.

What percentage of your psychophysical energy do you invest in your recreational activities? Use the 0 to 100 scale to estimate the amount of energy you devote to them. Remember the total amount of energy for all of your lifestyle parts cannot exceed 100.

What would you like to change about your recreational activities? What activities would you like to add or subtract? If you are uncertain then say so.

How important are making these changes to your lifestyle right now? Use the 0 to 100 scale where 0 equals "not important now" and 100 equals "critically important."

When you have completed the worksheet, write your "recreation net" number on the Recreation Net line of the form on page 25.

Net Lifestyle Satisfaction Worksheet

Date:
PART: MY RECREATION
A. Define your recreation:
B. Rate your recreation satisfaction: (0 = none; 100 = high)
C. Rate the importance of your recreation: (0 = none; 100 = high)
D. Percentage of your energy consumed by recreation: (0 to 100%)
Changes you would like to make in your recreation: □ none □ uncertain
E. Rate the importance of these changes/uncertainty: (0 = none; 100 = high)

RECREATION Summary

(_____ + _____) x _____ = _____

  Satisfaction rating   Importance rating   Energy percentage   RECREATION
  (Section B score)   (Section C score)   (Section D score)   NET

CHANGES

□ none

□ yes

□ uncertain

Importance Rating _____
   (Section E)

Money

Use the worksheet on page 27 as you consider the following questions. Record your answers in the appropriate space on the worksheet. Money is a fundamental part of everyone's lifestyle. Money is a system for assigning value to things. Indirectly money also assigns value to our relationships with others. It is therefore very important to think through your relationship to money.

How much money does your lifestyle require? How much savings do you have and do you want to have? Are your expenses more, less, or equal to your income? Is your level of debt too high? How much money would you like to earn each year? What is your current income? What was your income five years ago?

How satisfied are you with your relationship with money? Use the 0 to 100 scale.

How important is money in your current lifestyle? Use the 0 to 100 scale.

How much of your psychophysical energy is devoted to earning, spending, investing, and otherwise managing your money? Use the 0 to 100 percentage scale.

What would you like to change in your relationship with money? Do you want more or less money? Less debt? More spending? Are you wasting your money? Be as specific as you can. How important is it to make the changes specified above? Use the 0 to 100 scale.

When you have completed the worksheet, write your "money net" number on the Money Net line of the form on page 27.

Net Lifestyle Satisfaction Worksheet

Date:
PART: MY MONEY
A. Define your money:
B. Rate your money satisfaction: (0 = none; 100 = high)
C. Rate the importance of your money: (0 = none; 100 = high)
D. Percentage of your energy consumed by money: (0 to 100%)
Changes you would like to make in your money: □ none □ uncertain
E. Rate the importance of these changes/uncertainty: (0 = none; 100 = high)

MONEY Summary

(_____ + _____) x _____ = _____
Satisfaction rating   Importance rating   Energy percentage   MONEY NET
(Section B score)   (Section C score)   (Section D score)

CHANGES
□ none
□ yes
□ uncertain

Importance Rating _____
(Section E)

Future Plans

All of us have hopes, dreams, and aspirations of some kind, from winning the lottery to winning a promotion. To what extent have you turned any of your hopes into a plan for making them a reality? Think about what your hopes and dreams are today. Which of them have you developed into a plan of action? Perhaps you haven't done this for any of them. Use the worksheet on page 29 as you consider the following questions. Record your answers in the appropriate space on the worksheet.

Describe a current hope or dream and the plan you have developed to make it a reality. Be as specific as you can.

After you have read your plan, how much satisfaction does it give you to imagine making your plan a reality? Use the 0 to 100 scale to rate your satisfaction. If you do not have any current plans, give this a 0 rating and skip to section E on the worksheet.

How important is it for your future to make your plan work? Use the 0 to 100 scale.

What amount of energy are you currently devoting to implementing your plans? If you are not devoting any of your psychophysical energy to implementing your plans then rate this 0. Remember all of your energy ratings cannot exceed 100 after they are summed.

Is there anything you would like to change about your plans? Would you like to develop a new one? Would you like to develop new goals? Would you like to rethink your dreams and hopes? Be as specific as you can. How important is it for you to make these changes in the next few weeks? Use the 0 to 100 scale to rate this.

When you have completed the worksheet, write your "future plans net" number on the Future Plans Net line of the form on page 29.

Net Lifestyle Satisfaction Worksheet

Date:
PART: MY FUTURE PLANS
A. Define your future plans:
B. Rate your future plans satisfaction: (0 = none; 100 = high)
C. Rate the importance of your future plans: (0 = none; 100 = high)
D. Percentage of your energy consumed by future plans: (0 to 100%)
Changes you would like to make in your future plans: ☐ none ☐ uncertain
E. Rate the importance of these changes/uncertainty: (0 = none; 100 = high)

FUTURE Summary

(_____ + _____) x _____ = _____
Satisfaction rating Importance rating Energy percentage FUTURE PLAN
(Section B score)   (Section C score)   (Section D score)   NET

CHANGES

☐ none

☐ yes

☐ uncertain

Importance Rating _____
   (Section E)

Spiritual Connections and Values

Use the worksheet on page 31 as you consider the following questions. Record your answers in the appropriate space on the worksheet. What, if any, are your spiritual beliefs and values? What do you believe about the origin of the universe and of life on earth? What do believe is the purpose or value of life? Is death the end of an individual's being? Is there a larger purpose to why you live each day the way you do? Or is life without meaning or purpose for you? Describe your spiritual beliefs and values as simply as you can.

How much satisfaction do these beliefs bring to your life? Use your 0 to 100 scale. If you do not have any spiritual beliefs that you can define, then rate this a 0.

How important are your spiritual beliefs and values to your everyday life? Rate this on the 0 to 100 scale.

How much energy do you devote to your spiritual experiences? Do you meditate, pray, attend organized rituals, or perform other activities that relate to your spiritual life? Use the 0 to 100 scale to rate this and remember all of these ratings must add up to 100.

What, if anything, would you like to change about your spiritual beliefs and values? Do you need further education, reading, or other experiences? Be as specific as you can. How important are these changes to your life? Rate this on your 0 to 100 scale.

When you have completed the worksheet, write your "spirituality net" number on the Spirituality Net line of the form on page 31.

Net Lifestyle Satisfaction Worksheet

Date:

PART: MY SPIRITUAL BELIEFS AND VALUES

A. Define your spiritual beliefs and values:

B. Rate your spirituality satisfaction: (0 = none: 100 = high)

C. Rate the importance of your spirituality: (0 = none; 100 = high)

D. Percentage of your energy consumed by spirituality: (0 to 100%)

Changes you would like to make in your spirituality:

□ none

□ uncertain

E. Rate the importance of these changes/uncertainty: (0 = none; 100 = high)

SPIRITUALITY Summary

(_____ + _____) x _____ = _____
  Satisfaction rating   Importance rating   Energy percentage   SPIRITUALITY
  (Section B score)   (Section C score)   (Section D score)   NET

CHANGES

□ none

□ yes

□ uncertain

Importance Rating _____
   (Section E)

Self-Development

The final area is self-development. By this I mean activities whose major or sole focus is the improvement of your psychological functioning as a person. Reducing your stress levels, understanding your development as a person, soothing past psychological trauma, or developing new behavioral skills are all part of what I mean by self-development. Losing weight, exercising more, managing your heart disease or diabetes better, or giving up an addictive activity are specific examples of self-development. Use the worksheet on page 33 as you consider the following questions. Record your answers in the appropriate space on the worksheet.

Describe your two most important self-development activities and goals. Be specific. If you do not have any self-development goals, then say so.

How much satisfaction does the prospect of achieving these goals give you? Rate this on your 0 to 100 scale. If you do not have any self-development goals then rate this a 0.

How important are these goals to your life? Rate them on your 0 to 100 scale.

How much energy are you currently devoting (*not* would like to devote) to the achievement of these goals? Think carefully about this. A good way to estimate your energy allocation is to ask yourself how much time you devote to achieving these goals. Use your 0 to 100 scale.

How would you like to change, add to, or modify your self-development goals? If you do not have any goals, then you can speculate about what kind of goals you would like to set for yourself instead. Rate how important achieving your goals is to you at this time in your life. If you do not have any goals rate this 0.

When you have completed the worksheet, write your "self-development net" number on the Self-Development Net line of the form on page 33.

Net Lifestyle Satisfaction Worksheet

Date:

PART: MY SELF-DEVELOPMENT

A. Define your self-development:

B. Rate your self-development satisfaction: (0 = none; 100 = high)

C. Rate the importance of your self-development: (0 = none; 100 = high)

D. Percentage of your energy consumed by self-development: (0 to 100%)

Changes you would like to make in your self-development:

□ none

□ uncertain

E. Rate the importance of these changes/uncertainty: (0 = none; 100 = high)

SELF DEVELOPMENT Summary

(_____ + _____) x _____ = _____

Satisfaction rating   Importance rating   Energy percentage   SELF-DEVELOPMENT
(Section B score)   (Section C score)   (Section D score)   NET

CHANGES

□ none

□ yes

□ uncertain

Importance Rating _____
   (Section E)

Naming Your Addiction(s)

Now that you have assessed your lifestyle's satisfaction, it's time to name your addiction. The major focus of this book is substances such as alcohol, cocaine, heroin, crack, pot, speed, and so forth. There are other addictive activities, such as gambling, sex, self-mutilation, overeating, smoking, and self-starvation. Very often co-addictions and cross addictions exist. In many cases one addictive activity is a trigger for another. For example, having a few drinks at the local bar sets up a cocaine connection. However, not all people who use an "addictive" activity get addicted. So, what then is the definition of being addicted to something? Unfortunately experts do not agree on the precise definition of any addiction. Our definition is a pretty good one, but there are variations and alternatives out there as well.

You're addicted to an activity if you can honestly answer "yes" to most of these items:

1. You cannot stop the activity for at least thirty continuous days.

2. When you do stop the activity you experience withdrawal symptoms.

3. Your consumption of the activity causes you to fail to meet your financial, family, work, or self-care responsibilities.

4. You find yourself frequently thinking about the next time that you can use your activity.

5. You find yourself using more and more of your activity—more frequent or a greater quantity.

6. People who know you well start to tell you that you are addicted.

7. You find yourself lying to other people about your activity.

8. You have to steal money to fund your activity.

9. You get arrested because of your activity.

10. You feel depressed or angry when you cannot engage in your activity for as little as a three-day period.

If you can answer "yes" to at least five of these questions with respect to your potentially addictive activity then chances are you are either addicted or well on your way to becoming addicted.

Your Addiction Intensity Score from the Introduction should also give you a good estimate of how severe your addiction has become. If you haven't filled it out yet please take a moment to do so now. You need to see the truth of your condition before you can do something about it.

With these criteria in mind, check off your addictive activities from the selection that follows:

Addictive Activities

- ☐ Heroin
- ☐ Alcohol
- ☐ Tobacco/smoking
- ☐ Cocaine
- ☐ Crack
- ☐ Marijuana
- ☐ Amphetamine
- ☐ Designer drugs
- ☐ LSD
- ☐ Other hallucinogens
- ☐ Painkillers
- ☐ Tranquilizers
- ☐ Inhalants
- ☐ Gambling
- ☐ Promiscuous sex
- ☐ Self-mutilation
- ☐ Self-starvation (anorexia)
- ☐ Gorging and purging (bulimia)
- ☐ Dangerous driving
- ☐ High-risk, dangerous situations (e.g., fights)
- ☐ Internet sex
- ☐ Other _____

Check over your list of addictive activities. Is it complete and one hundred percent honest?

Calculating the Cost of Your Addiction

The next step is to calculate how much your addiction is costing you. How is it affecting your lifestyle? The cost of an addiction goes beyond the monetary. It can have a significant social, professional, and family price tag. Be as honest as you can. Only you will see the results, so you do not have to hide anything from yourself.

My Addiction's Nonfinancial Costs

Check all the costs that apply to you.

□ Lost my driver's license

□ Lost my professional license (law, psychology, medicine, etc.)

□ Evicted from my home

□ In debt over my head

□ Lived in a shelter or was homeless on the street

□ Passed over for a promotion

□ Spent savings on my addiction

□ Spent time in jail due to my addiction

□ Stole things to finance my addiction

□ Sold sexual favors to finance my addiction

□ Arrested/charged with DWI, DUI, etc.

□ On probation due to my addiction

□ Involved in physical fights while under the influence

□ Got into accident (car, fall, injury, etc.) due to my addiction

□ Injured myself due to my addiction

□ Relationship with loved one damaged by my addiction

□ Lost friends due to my addiction

□ Put myself into high-risk situations to satisfy my addiction

□ Lost trust of friends and loved ones

□ Spent more time with my addiction than with my family

□ My health has been seriously harmed by my addiction

□ Lost my motivation to do healthy or productive activities

□ Lost jobs or a career because of my addiction

□ Tried to kill myself

□ Lied and manipulated loved ones to get money for my addiction

Count up the number checked and multiply it by 3. If you checked more than 10 items add 25 to your total. The maximum score is 100.

My total score is _____. Write your score on the form on page 38 as well.

The last step in the analysis of your lifestyle satisfaction is to calculate the monetary cost of your addiction. Use the Financial Loss Inventory to do this. Your calculation will not be absolutely accurate and that is okay. Just give it a little thought and try not to underestimate the dollar costs of your addiction. Be as honest as you can. It will benefit you greatly.

Financial Loss Inventory

Item	Total dollars spent ($)
Amount of money YOU spent on rehabs	$
Amount of money lost selling your possessions to get money	$
Amount of money YOU spent to buy your addictive substances	$
Amount of money YOU spent on transportation to get, use, or sell your substances	$
Amount of money YOU lost due to missing work, and losing promotions, raises, and so forth	$
Amount of money YOU lost due to not attending school	$
Amount of money YOU spent on legal fees, fines, and probation	$
Amount of money YOU spent on medical bills, ER visits, etc.	$
GRAND TOTAL	$

Write in all of your Lifestyle NET ratings:

Net Lifestyle Satisfaction Summary Sheet

Lifestyle Net Scores	Net Rating	My Comments
WORK (from page 17)		
FAMILY (from page 19)		
FRIENDS (from page 21)		
INTIMATES (from page 23)		
RECREATION (from page 25)		
MONEY (from page 27)		
FUTURE PLANS (from page 29)		
SPIRITUAL (from page 31)		
SELF-DEVELOPMENT (from page 33)		
A. TOTAL NET VALUE (Add up all of the above numbers—maximum score is 200)		
B. MINUS MY ADDICTION'S NONFINANCIAL COSTS (From page 36)		
MY NET LIFESTYLE SATISFACTION (Subtract B from A)		
Dollar Cost of My Addiction (Your total from page 37)	$	

If your Net Lifestyle Satisfaction score is less than 125 then it suggests that you are not getting the satisfaction you want from your life. If your score is less than 100 then it is clear that you are definitely not satisfied with your life as it is. If you score less than 75 then immediate changes are needed before things get worse. If you score above 125 then you are fairly satisfied with your life. If you score above 150 you are very satisfied with the way your life is going.

If your total addiction costs exceed one-fifth of your annual income then you have a serious habit that, regardless of your current lifestyle satisfaction, will catch up with you one day soon.

My Preferred Lifestyle

Now that you have figured out how satisfied you are with your current lifestyle and how much your addiction is costing, you are ready to make a decision about whether you want to modify your addictive activities in any way. To help you reach this decision, think about what your preferred lifestyle would be like. Spend some time considering the following questions. On separate sheets of paper, write the most detailed answers you can.

1. Think back for a moment to a time before you were involved with your addictive activities. How old were you? Where were you living? What were you doing? Was this a good time in your life? Write about your recollections of this pre-addiction time. Keep your summary to about 100 words.

2. Describe an accomplishment that you are particularly proud of. Think carefully about it and describe it in detail. Why are you so proud of this accomplishment?

3. How would you describe the kind of person you think you really are? If you had to write a fifty-word summary describing yourself, what would you say? How would your closest friends describe you? Write your answers in detail.

4. In what ways have your actions fallen short of the standards you have set for yourself? Of who you really are? How have you disappointed yourself?

5. How do your loved ones perceive you? How does the way they see you differ from how you perceive yourself? (This is a tough question to answer.)

6. How much does the difference between your view of yourself and your loved ones' view of you trouble you?

Take a moment to read over all of your answers to the previous questions. After you have done this look back over your lifestyle ratings, and then review the costs of your addiction. Have you been as honest as you can be? Are you satisfied with the effort you put into completing your analysis? If so move on to the next chapter. If not, re-do the part of your analysis that you are not happy with.

It's time to put it all together.

- My Net Lifestyle Satisfaction is _____.

- The Financial Cost of My Addiction is $_____.

- Do I have a preferred vision for my life? □ Yes   □ No

Are you satisfied with the addictions in your lifestyle?

◻ Yes

◻ No

◻ I'm not sure

The next chapter will help you to clarify your judgment.

3
Ready or Not

Conventional wisdom says that a person must "hit bottom" before she is ready to surrender to the need to give up her addictive activities. But "hitting bottom" does not mean that your life has irreparably fallen apart. Nor does hitting bottom guarantee that you will decide to get clean. A walk through any major U.S. city will bring you into contact with many people who have hit bottom—for good. What hitting bottom does is tip your lifestyle satisfaction into a noticeably negative enough direction for you to wake up to what you are doing to yourself, your loved ones, and your future. The operative word in this last sentence is *noticeably*. And the only person who needs to notice the decline is you. It's an inside thing. It really doesn't matter how many times people preach at you or beg you or love you or threaten you—what matters is what you feel inside. If you are satisfied with the addictions in your lifestyle then no one is going to persuade you to feel otherwise. It goes back to what we said in chapter one—that you, my friend, are in control to the end. This is true even if that end is The End. This is a sobering thought (no pun intended).

As we noted earlier a majority of substance users (including those who use drugs, alcohol, and cigarettes) stop using on their own. Some studies show that up to 75 percent of people who are addicted to a substance stop on their own—without entering a formal treatment program. How do they do it? Fifty-seven percent do it by weighing the pros and cons of continued use. These people do not use a single bad experience to reach their decisions. They follow an evaluation process similar to the one we laid out for you in the last chapter. They weigh the good and bad aspects of their lifestyles and how their addictive activities are affecting it. They take the time to think about the quality of their lives and whether they deserve better. After they evaluate, they make their decisions—to change or not to change.

If you have completed the exercises in the previous chapter, then you are ready to make a decision. Here are your choices.

Ready for Recovery

This means that you've decided that enough is enough. It's time to reduce or eliminate addictive activities. You are ready to make a full commitment to change things. You know what you need to do and are ready to do it.

Real People, Real Experiences

Tim is a thirty-nine-year-old cocaine addict who has been in and out of rehabs and detox units since the age of nineteen. After nearly dying of an overdose he decided to get himself clean and sober. Tim slowly worked himself into changing his behavior. The process started after Tim underwent ERP therapy and went to Narcotics Anonymous meetings. He also started to reach out to others and allowed them to help him. He sought out help from his sponsor, friends, family, and therapist whenever he feared for his recovery. He worked with his therapist on long-standing family problems that he had avoided for many years. Tim was very open to information, suggestions, and feedback—he no longer believed that his way was the only way. Tim was ready for recovery.

Ready But Unsure How

You are ready to make the commitment to change, but you aren't quite sure of how to go about getting started. You need to do some thinking and legwork to figure this out.

Real People, Real Experiences

Liz is a thirty-four-year-old alcoholic. She too was in and out of treatment facilities since her late teens. Liz decided to get clean and sober only after Child Protective Services took her three children away from her because of neglect. After this happened Liz realized that her children were more important to her than booze. But Liz did not know how to go about getting started. She called a number of doctors and facilities and asked questions. She contacted her insurance company for referrals. In the interim she started to attend Alcoholics Anonymous daily.

She admitted herself to a rehab program where she began to look at her past as motivating her addiction to alcohol. She learned to see the connection between her dysfunctional childhood and her vulnerability to addiction. Liz began psychotherapy to learn to overcome past trauma so she could stay in recovery. Eventually, she regained custody of both her life and her children.

Continuing Use, But Open to Feedback

Things aren't too bad. You'd like to get more information on whether you should consider reducing your addictive activities, but for now you're going to continue as before.

Real People, Real Experiences

Jimmy was a twenty-one-year-old heroin addict. He began his drug addiction at age eighteen. Jimmy was cool and attractive. He knew himself and had nothing to hide. Jimmy honestly said at admission that he was going to use heroin again and was not ready to give it up—he only needed a break. In rehab Jimmy met other people struggling with addictions. They talked to him about how their lives changed for the better once they made an attempt at living a sober life. These conversations helped Jimmy to realize that it is possible to enjoy life without heroin. He still held to his position that he would use again, but the "seeds" were planted in his mind. Recovery often begins with small steps.

Continuing to Use, Will Listen to Feedback If Pushed

Things seem fine. The benefits of your addictive activities seem to balance the negatives. Your perception is that nothing really needs to change, but you can see that if things get worse you may have to reconsider your position.

Real People, Real Experiences

Jaime, a nineteen-year-old heroin addict from a very well-off family, had been in treatment for her addiction for about a year. Whenever the topic of heroin was brought up Jaime would smile and get a gleam in her eye—she really enjoyed her heroin high. Jaime knew that heroin was "bad" for her but she was honest when she said that she wasn't ready to quit using it. Her parents insisted that she remain in treatment and she went along with this because they held the purse strings. In her rehab groups, ERP sessions, and psychotherapy she explored her addiction to heroin and how it really controlled her life in ways that were not as much fun as she thought. She began to think that maybe she should quit. Other patients' stories of how heroin ruined their lives started to get to her, but she could not fully accept the fact that heroin would do the same to her. Jaime remained on the fence about her addiction and leaned toward using again once she "completed" rehab.

Going to Use Right Now

You judge things to be pretty positive. There is no reason in your mind to stop or even cut back. You enjoy using and you intend to continue to do so—maybe as soon as you finish reading this.

Real People, Real Experiences

Ricky, a thirty-five-year-old cocaine user, has been in and out of rehab several times since his addiction began seven years ago. Ricky entered his last rehab facing seven felony charges. Ricky was not ready to give up his cocaine and instead was willing to gamble on getting out of the charges. His family couldn't understand why Ricky did not see what he was doing to himself. He used to be a successful stockbroker making a six-figure income. And now he was an overage adolescent. Ricky is still using three to four times per week. Recently he violated his probation and is looking at doing some jail time. The court, probation officer, therapist, friends, doctor, and family cannot persuade him to get off his path of self-destruction. Ricky is a committed addict and he is not ready to change.

So Where Are You?

Take a moment to reflect on each of these options and to ask yourself which option best describes the place you find yourself in today. If you think you are ready to make a commitment to cut back or stop—great, we're ready to help you get going. If you aren't ready to do anything, that's fine too. Choice is what life is all about. If you are satisfied with your life and your addictions, then it is a choice you've made.

You might be wondering, why do some people choose not to stop or cut back? There are as many reasons as there are people, but the most common fall into five categories.

1. Other people are paying for your addiction—enablers. If you have people in your life who are willing to cover for the negative consequences of your addiction then you have less incentive to change. When no one is ready to bail you out you will be more likely to change.

2. It's still exciting, fun, and a great escape. If you enjoy it, then you have no reason to stop.

3. Others are pushing too hard for you to stop. No one likes to be told what to do—addicts least of all. The more they push the harder you resist.

4. You are still think you are young and immortal—you are immune to the negative lifestyle and health risks of addiction. This is a common reason among younger people. Highly successful people also think this way too. The passing of time will teach us otherwise.

5. Most frightening of all reasons is that you do not care whether you live or die. You have given up on having a "normal life." Your brain has become hooked on your addictive substance and you cannot resist its call to use because you no longer care about yourself—you hate who and what you are. You have lost all hope and see only addiction in your future. Everything is dark; addiction is the only "light."

Your lifestyle balance sheet may be telling you that it is time to stop, but the plain old fact may be that you love the stuff (and all that goes with it) too much to quit. Somewhere in a quiet corner of your mind you may be thinking, "I need to do something," but the reality is that you're just too hooked to make your mouth ask for help. If this describes where you are, then perhaps it will help you to know that it will probably take legal problems, a serious health crisis, or the death of someone close to you to get you to do what you cannot do on your own right now. Get help!

We know there is someone who you could turn to even now who could help you find the help you need. All you need do is ask. Think about it. Maybe you will find the strength to ask.

The Next Step

If you decide to make a commitment to changing, then read on. If not, you are certainly welcome to continue reading along as well.

4

The Six ERP Recovery Steps

You now know that you are committed to making a major change in the way you are living with addiction. In this chapter you are going figure out how to do it. There are six ERP Recovery steps to cover.

Commitment

Decision creates determination and commitment. Once they've made a commitment people do not make straight-line changes. They zigzag their way along. Relapses are the rule and not the exception. Changing behavior takes time. Rarely do we change in a single step. We take small steps. We move forward and then we fall back. If we beat ourselves up when we fall back, that's how we fail. If we accept setbacks as a normal part of the self-change process, then we can motivate a renewal of effort to press ahead. So you need to realize that self-change is like the ocean tide as it comes in. Gradually it covers more and more of the beach. Your self-change efforts will inevitably cover more and more of your addictive behavior until none of it remains. Picking yourself up, dusting yourself off, and stepping up to the plate again and again is the key to success. In a word, success is determination. You may suffer a setback, you may even fall flat on your face, but you must resolve that you will never, never give up—you will succeed.

"I am committed to reducing my addictions." This is your mantra. Make it part of your everyday mind-set and you will gradually transform your life.

Setting up a Support Network

Out with the old and in with the new. Your old addiction "friends" cannot help you in your quest to get clean. Regrettably, they are part of your dysfunctional past. Finding supporters—people who will help you to remain motivated—is your next task. Fact: People who succeed at getting clean do so because they have at least one person they love (and who loves them) who really wants them to get addiction free. They stay clean partly because they do not want to lose this person's love.

The next chapter will cover ways that you can set up a secure and effective support network to reinforce your addiction-free lifestyle.

Learn to Kill Your Cravings with ERP

In the last five years, a breakthrough method has emerged that can help your to kill your cravings and thereby control the impulse to get high. The conventional advice to avoid the people, places, and things associated with substance abuse is very sound. The problem is that it is not possible to totally avoid these potential triggers. Sooner or later virtually one hundred percent of former abusers are exposed to powerful substance using triggers. And a very high percentage of them—about seventy-five percent—eventually succumb to their seductive song.

Recognizing the inevitability of trigger exposure, the clinical team at SLS Health developed ERP therapy. ERP therapy can help you reduce the seductive power of triggering stimuli. Psychologists have long known that neutral stimuli that become physically or temporally associated with addictive substances acquire the power to stimulate a user's impulse to use. Once these stimuli acquire this conditioned power, exposure to them triggers an impulse to consume the associated substance. Through a therapeutic procedure called exposure response prevention (ERP) the power of a stimulus to trigger an impulse to use can be extinguished. Extinguishing the power of a drug—or alcohol-associated stimulus (called *extinction*)—does not *erase* the association but helps keep it in a dormant state. It will remain dormant as long as the stimulus is not again associated with the use of the addictive substance. For extinction to occur, a person must be exposed to the triggering stimuli and be prevented from using. Merely refraining from use without exposure to triggering stimuli will *not* extinguish the trigger's ability to evoke an impulse to use. To control the impulse, you have to be exposed to powerful triggers *and* not use. Repeated exposure is needed for complete response extinction to occur.

An example may help illustrate this process in action. Consider a person who has an irrational fear of dogs. If this person is afraid of dogs and she avoids going near a dog, her fear will persist for years. The passage of time by itself will not eliminate the fear. The only thing that will eliminate the fear is a series of pleasant contacts with dogs. By exposing herself to dogs and associating that contact with the *absence* of anything bad happening, she will gradually extinguish the fear of dogs.

We have developed photo-guided and therapist-guided forms of ERP. This book covers the photo-guided form, which you can safely self-administer. We will show you how to self-administer photo-based ERP in chapter 7.

Reclaiming Your Lifestyle

Once you have learned to kill your cravings with ERP, you can focus even more effectively on reclaiming your lifestyle. Why is it important to reclaim your lifestyle? There are three major reasons: (1) you cannot associate with your abuser friends anymore; (2) the "activity void" created by giving up an abusing lifestyle needs to be filled; and (3) you need to repair the damage your addiction has done.

The first reason is fairly obvious. The old party friends who are still partying will trigger you to use. You can talk with them and tell them that you are stopping. You can ask them to not trigger you. They may even say they'd be glad to help you. But it won't work! Being around your old using friends is a very powerful incentive to use. If you want to stay addiction free there is only one thing you can do: cut the ties completely.

The second reason is a little subtler. People who develop a powerful addiction spend a lot of time getting, preparing, and using their substances of choice. As your addiction progresses, more and more of your lifestyle is consumed by it. Work, play, family life, recreation, and friends all take a distant second place to your addiction. Once you commit to ending the addiction, a huge void opens up. This void needs to be filled with healthy, self-esteem enhancing activities.

Finally, addiction damages and destroys the lifestyle of the people in its grasp. A major part of redesigning your lifestyle involves repairing it. Repair can be a humbling thing to do at times, but it will relieve you of your burden of remorse and guilt.

In chapter 8 we'll help you do these three things.

Guard Your Health and Your Recovery

Love yourself better than anyone else does. This is the best advice we can give you. At the core of every recovery is someone who finds out that they really do care about and love themselves. It takes the love of another to help you see this at first, but once you open you eyes and heart to who you really are, the change can take place. Without self-love recovery is temporary. With self-love (and self-respect) anything within your ability is possible. Chapter 9 helps you explore and apply these ideas in greater depth.

Enjoy the Results

The last step is a lot of fun. Enjoy the results of what you have accomplished. It is all too easy to feel really bad about your addiction and what it did to you and to those who love you. It may take you a couple of years to clean up the damage you did to your life, but it shouldn't take you that long to start enjoying the fact that you are accomplishing what you set out to do. Enjoying the results of your recovery will energize it and keep it rolling along smoothly. The last chapter of the book talks more about this.

5

Your Support Network

Okay, let's get to work building a really good support network. This chapter's main task is to help you figure out how to recruit the members of your support network. Without a strong support network, your chances of a successful recovery are very low. We want to repeat this. You cannot succeed in remaining clean and sober unless you have a very strong support group! For most addicts, organizations such as AA (Alcoholics Anonymous) or NA (Narcotics Anonymous) are an absolutely necessary part of recovery. Without healthy and consistent support there is no recovery for seriously addicted people.

Who should belong to your new support network? Potential members can be found among the people you already know and in community resource groups:

- Local support groups (such as AA and NA)

- Family

- Friends

- Lovers

- Professionals

- The Internet

- Religious organizations

Who should *not* be a part of your support network? Here are a few people who need to be excluded:

- Old drug and alcohol buddies

- Dealers

- Bar buddies

- Family members who are very negative about you

- People who still indulge in what you are addicted to

Family at Home

Your primary support network is composed of the people you live with. If you cannot count on the support of everyone you live with, you could be facing some rough going at home. You can solidify home front support by clearly explaining to each person that you are attempting to overcome your addiction and that you need his or her support. If you get a negative response from someone, calmly ask him to explain his reasons. Chances are he will say that he has heard you claim you were going to quit before, but you didn't. If this is true acknowledge the truth of it. The key here is to be emotionally honest and to take responsibility for your past behavior. You cannot simply blame the past on the fact that you were (and are) an addict. That is a half-truth. Accept this person's criticisms and anger. Tell him that you do not blame him for his skepticism, and ask him to avoid being negative about your current effort. Ask him to wait and see how you do. Your goal: If someone cannot give you positive support then ask him to stay neutral (until he sees that you are serious).

Community Support Groups

Community-based support groups can be a valuable source of support for some people. Groups such as AA and NA have been around for many years and have helped thousands of people maintain their sobriety. Alcoholics Anonymous chapters can be found in virtually every city and town across the United States. AA was founded in the late 1890s and is based on the twelve steps of recovery. AA requires that its members pledge themselves to total sobriety—zero tolerance for drugs and alcohol. New members are expected to complete ninety meetings in ninety days to help them through the initial period of withdrawal. We have found that it takes a newly sober person at least thirty days to feel comfortable with an AA group meeting. The first few meetings feel awkward. You need to stick it out and find a sponsor. It does get easier once you accept your addiction for what it has become: something you cannot control. Stay with AA, because AA has saved many people's lives. To find the group nearest to you call AA at 212-870-3400.

For those of you who do not want to deal with the spiritual aspects of AA, there is an alternative in Rational Recovery or RR. RR uses a logical counseling approach to help its members stay addiction free. RR is based in part on a form of psychotherapy called Rational Emotive Therapy or RET. RET views dysfunctional behavior as caused by irrational beliefs that go unexamined and therefore automatically produce undesirable behavior. By identifying and then challenging these irrational beliefs you can free yourself more easily of the dysfunctional behaviors connected to them. To get more information about RR you can contact them at 800-303-2873.

NA or Narcotics Anonymous was founded to help people with drug problems. They follow AA's twelve-step program and welcome people from all walks of life. You can contact NA by calling 818-773-9999.

You can use a community-based support group to strengthen your motivation to remain free of addiction. During the early stages of recovery many people feel cut off from old "friends." A community support group helps to fill this void. You can make new friends and learn how other people manage their recoveries. Of course, attending a support group isn't for everyone. However, if you do not have other people to lean on in time of need, then you should consider putting a support group into your support network.

Family and Friends

Whom do you trust and who trusts you? This is a "chicken and egg" question. Your past addictive behavior has probably burned more than a few bridges with loved ones. You're going to need support from some of them to succeed. But the past has them feeling just a little suspicious. How do you bridge the "trust gap" to gain the support you need? No simple answers here.

The best approach to take with the people you have burned in the past is to sincerely ask for forgiveness and to make amends. This involves making a list of family and friends you've hurt, how you have hurt them, and why you did what you did. The next step is the hard one: the apology. Go to each one and tell them that you know you hurt them. You cannot change what you did to them. You need to accept the fact that they have every right to be angry with you—to even hate you, but you are asking for their forgiveness (and help). If doing this sounds tough to you, that's because it is! However, if you can do this, you will reap a tremendous benefit. You'll unload a lot of guilt and self-hate—and gain some much-needed emotional support.

If you decide to try to make amends, what kind of response can you expect? The first thing to know is what *not* to expect. The people you've hurt are very unlikely to forgive and completely forget the past. This is especially true if you've made similar promises in the past to your spouse, parents, or close friends. In fact, it is unrealistic to expect that anyone close to you would let his guard down totally. A more reasonable expectation is that they will appreciate your apology and desire to make amends. They will be willing to trust you, but only as long as they see your recovery continue. You should welcome the opportunity to make amends by verifying for your loved ones the ongoing truth of your recovery. Regaining the trust of those you love is a critically important part of recovery. Without their trust your recovery will eventually be jeopardized.

Not everyone will offer you a "trust but verify" response. There is a chance that some of your family and friends will reject what you have to say. If someone you've apologized to does this, avoid getting angry or discouraged. If you have lied to her, stolen from her, and repeatedly broken promises to her, perhaps she has good reason to disbelieve you now. Validate her right to reject your apology and move on. That is all you can do for now. Let your actions show her that you are indeed serious about your current attempt at recovery. Perhaps she will come around.

Finally, there will be people who will accept your apology, but who will remain skeptical of your ability to follow through on your recovery. They are unlikely to trust you anytime soon for fear that you will use their trust to enable your habit. But they will take a wait-and-see attitude toward you. This puts the ball clearly in your court. It's up to you to show through your actions (and not with slick words) that you are recovering for the long term.

If you allow the skeptical attitudes of loved ones to anger or hurt you, then you are living in a fantasy world. If you have hurt them with your addictions in the past, then they have every right to doubt you now. If you want their love and support now, you owe them an apology and a full effort to make amends for what you did to them. Part of making amends is to respectfully accept their doubt and skepticism of you and to show them by your hard-won actions that you can once again be worthy of their trust. There is no other way.

Lovers

Lovers are a special group of people whom we consider separately from family and friends. A lover is your romantic partner in life. It is the person whom you trust and care about the most. It is the person you are sexually intimate with. It is the person who can be your greatest supporter or greatest enabler.

Lovers are biased to believe that you will get clean and stay clean. They are generally slow to see the signs of relapse. Their affection for you often blurs their perception of what you are up to. Their tolerance for your "white lies" and other deceptions is also high. Bottom line: You can BS your lover for a long time before you finally reach his or her limit.

Research has shown that having at least one close person who really wants you to stay in recovery is a critical piece of being successful. (Now, this "close person" does not *have* to be a lover. He or she could also be a friend, parent, brother, sister, or clergy member.) Without such a person your chances for success drop significantly. This brings us back to your lover. By manipulating your lover with lies, omissions, deceptions, and rages, you insure your own failure. Furthermore, you risk having them give up on you entirely. But you need that one special person who will support you through your recovery no matter what. So this is your dilemma: deceive your lover and you fail. Tell your lover the truth and you risk exposing your tricks for using on the sly.

The smart move is to be totally honest with your lover. Tell them when you are craving. Tell them if you've slipped. Don't leave anything out. Be so honest that it scares you. Show them that you are totally serious about staying with the program. Never deceive them. Let them be there for you. They want to do this for you. They want you to succeed. By being honest with them your success will be virtually guaranteed.

The exception to the above advice: if your lover is an addict, a chronic enabler, or both. If this is the case, you must end the relationship at once. Your recovery will fail—it cannot possibly succeed—unless you do so. You will probably need the support of a professional therapist to do this.

Professional Counseling

Most people who have addictive problems also have associated psychological problems, such as depression, anxiety, attention deficit disorder, or a history of psychotrauma (such as abuse, rape, or a very dysfunctional family life). In addition to dealing with their addiction, they must also face the prospect of feeling their lives again. They must also face the people whom they have hurt because of their addiction.

As your recovery progresses you will begin to feel these problems more than you did while you were actively addicted. As you know, one of the benefits of being addicted is that the pleasure of the high and the discomfort of the crash effectively numb the negative feelings associated with these psychological problems (this is sometimes called "self-medicating"). One of the major reasons people relapse is that they cannot handle their psychological feelings without their addictions. If this describes your situation then you need to seek out professional counseling to manage these problems before they trigger a relapse. Getting most recovering addicts to a therapist is like getting a little kid to take her medicine. So we aren't going to preach about how good therapy is for you or how good you'll feel once it starts working. We are just going to say that it can't hurt to check it out. To find a good therapist near you, click into our Web site at *www.slshealth.com*.

If you are not ready to consult a therapist, then consider consulting your company's Employee Assistance Program counselor, your priest, rabbi, minister, or guru. They can be helpful sources of confidential, free counseling.

If you consult a professional therapist you can expect to spend at least six to twelve months in once-per-week counseling to achieve a useful outcome.

The Internet

The World Wide Web is alive and well everywhere. It has countless resources available to the person in recovery. It can provide you with information on chat groups, ways to make new friends, and ways to fill your empty hours. It can be a godsend to someone in recovery. If you do not own a computer, go out and buy one (they can be had for as little as five hundred dollars) with the money you are saving from not feeding your addiction. Plug it into your telephone, sign on to America Online or another service provider for about twenty dollars per month, click on Netscape or Explorer (they come with your computer), and you're online. It is that simple. A great book to read on how to get online quickly and easily is the internet for dummies.

Once you are online, finding information about addiction, treatment, and recovery is easy. All you need to do is click on the search button of your browser software. This will take you to a search engine such as Excite, Yahoo, or Netscape. Then type in the key words "addiction," "treatment," "recovery." Click "go" and you will see a list of hundreds of sites where you can find all kinds of information and help. Some of the sites we recommend as starting points are listed in the Resources section on page 131.

Religious Organizations

Most people who develop a severe addiction conduct a spiritual review of their lives. Some come to realize that God—however they understand this to be—has helped to keep them alive. Others regain a faith they once had in happier times. Still others find a faith they never had. Of course, not everyone in recovery finds religion. But almost all do consider what the larger purpose and deeper meaning of their lives are. If you find comfort in a community of fellow believers, then seek out their support and love for your recovery journey. If you wish to explore the meaning of your life from a nonreligious viewpoint, chapter 8 can help you with this.

Your Support Network

An ideal support group will include a close friend, lover, or family member who can be your primary supporter—that is, a person who is fully invested in your recovery. A primary supporter is someone who will be there for you through the difficult times of your recovery. It will also include a community support group such as AA, NA, or RR. Use of the Internet will help to fill up empty time and provide you with a wealth of helpful information, chat group support, and even online counseling. Finally, consulting a professional therapist will help you confront psychological issues that helped to fuel your addiction or were created as a result of it. This is a winning team: primary supporter, a support group, Internet use, and a professional therapist. Working as a team, you will greatly increase your chances for total recovery success.

Additional organized support group information can be obtained from the resources listed on pages 133–35.

6

ERP Your Cravings

In this chapter you will learn how to conduct your own ERP therapy session. ERP will help you to reduce and then nearly eliminate your desire to use alcohol and drugs. It is a scientifically validated therapy procedure that is based on years of behavioral research into how behaviors are conditioned to stimuli.

To learn how to use ERP you need to complete the following three steps:

1. Read and understand the theory behind ERP described in this chapter.

2. Practice deep breathing and body scan techniques, which are described in chapter 7, until you feel comfortable with them.

3. Run your first ERP session. You will need to run about twenty-five to thirty ERP sessions before you will significantly reduce your level of cravings. Each session will take about fifteen to twenty minutes.

The ERP Concept

Exposure response prevention (ERP) is a behavior therapy technology that reduces a person's predisposition to respond to a set of stimuli. For example, ERP has been used to treat phobias and compulsions by exposing a person to the phobic situation or thing (stimuli set) and then preventing them from executing their dysfunctional response (e.g., hand washing). We have applied this technique to the problem of substance abuse. One of the key hurdles a person must overcome to remain substance free is to refrain from substance consumption when exposed to stimuli (people, places, and things) formerly conditioned to their substance abuse. Failure to behaviorally ignore such conditioned stimuli is the primary cause of relapse among substance abusers. The range of stimuli conditioned as triggers of substance abuse is varied and individualized. There are, however, common triggers. The sensory stimuli associated with the substance of choice, its acquisition, and preparation for use, for instance, often become triggers. Secondly, there are the typical use settings, such as bars, time of day, or special event. Finally, emotional stressors, while more individualized, are another frequent trigger.

What Is a Craving?

When you use alcohol or drugs you introduce new chemicals into your brain. These chemicals compete with your normal brain chemicals for space in the "docking ports" at the ends of your nerve cells. The addictive chemicals are more powerful than your normal chemicals, so they tend to win this competition and dock with your nerve cells, causing them to fire in ways that let you feel high.

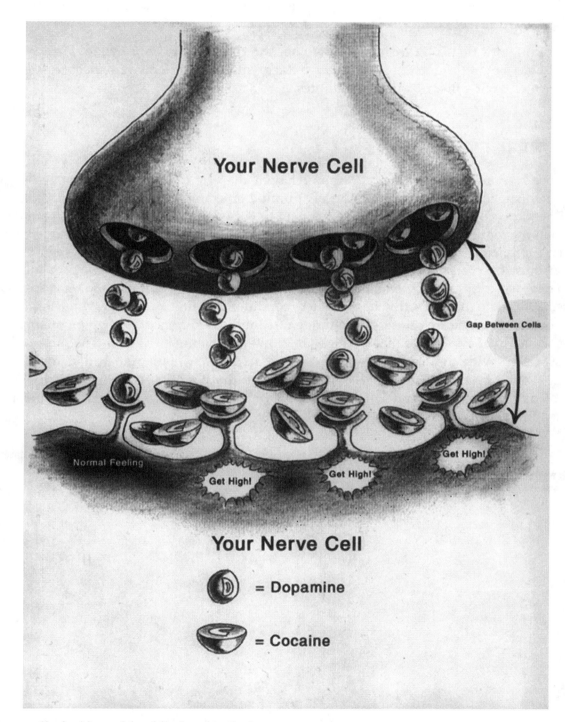

Nerve cells docking with addictive chemicals

As you get high more often your brain does two things. First, it produces fewer normal chemicals. It figures that as long as you are feeding it addictive chemicals it doesn't need to produce its normal chemicals, so it cuts back on their production. Your brain also does something else to manage this inflow of addictive chemicals. It closes down some of the docking ports. It realizes that its nerve cells are being overstimulated and that it needs to reduce the number of ports it keeps open in order to protect them from being overloaded.

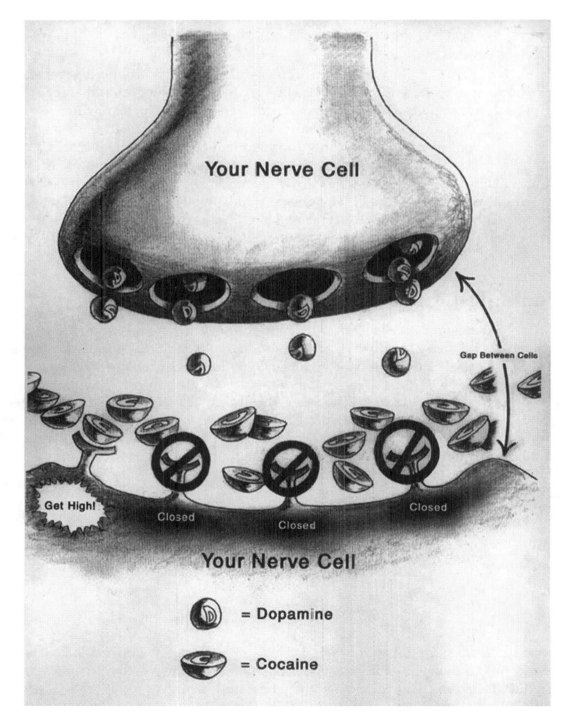

Brain adjusting itself by closing ports and decreasing normal chemical production

These brain changes have a big effect on you. It makes you use more and more of your addictive substance to try to achieve the same quality of high. But the more you use, the more adjustments your brain makes, and a vicious addictive cycle ensues.

When you stop "injecting" your brain with addictive chemicals, your normal brain chemicals remain at a lower rate of production. The production of normal chemicals does not rapidly increase to pre-addiction levels. The result is a *withdrawal syndrome* that makes you feel depressed, agitated, confused, physically sick, and so forth. Gradually, your brain will increase production of its normal chemicals and will reopen its docking ports, but this takes time. The time it takes depends on the addictive substance. A cocaine-addicted brain may take as long as six months (sometimes longer) before its production and docking ports fully return to normal.

As you come down from your last high, the addictive chemicals you ingested are broken down and removed by your brain's metabolism. But because your normal brain chemicals are in short supply you crave your substance of choice. Cravings are your nerve cells' way of screaming out for more drugs! Once you use again, the addictive chemicals dock with your nerve cells and satisfy their need for stimulation. If you do not use, your brain will gradually restart the production of normal chemicals. If you remain abstinent long enough, it will also start to reopen more of the nerve ending docking ports. If you ride out your "craving wave," you will find that it does subside. If you remain abstinent and ride out each wave as it comes, eventually your cravings will fade away (which means that your brain is repairing the damage caused by your addiction).

Psychological Conditioning

In addition to managing its chemistry, your brain also learns when, where, and how to expect to receive its dose of addictive chemicals. Powerful conditioning processes are set in motion each time you acquire, prepare, and use your addictive substance. This conditioning takes place independently of your will, and without your awareness. The pipe you use to smoke your pot, the brand of beer you drink, the appearance of your crack, your favorite bar, your drinking buddy's phone number, your bored feelings, your negative thinking, and many other stimuli become conditioned to your substance use habit chain. This conditioning process gives previously neutral stimuli the power to make you crave.

Stimulus	Conditional Response
Sight and smell of beer	Craving to drink
See crack pipe	Craving to smoke
See plastic bag	Craving to shoot heroin
Negative thinking	Craving to get high
Drug buddies	Craving to party

These stimuli can also cause your brain chemistry to change in anticipation of receiving its "injection" of addictive chemicals. The docking ports open and normal chemical production is reduced, inviting you to party with alcohol and drugs!

Alcohol

(See page 80 for instructions on how to use these photocards)

Cocaine

Crack

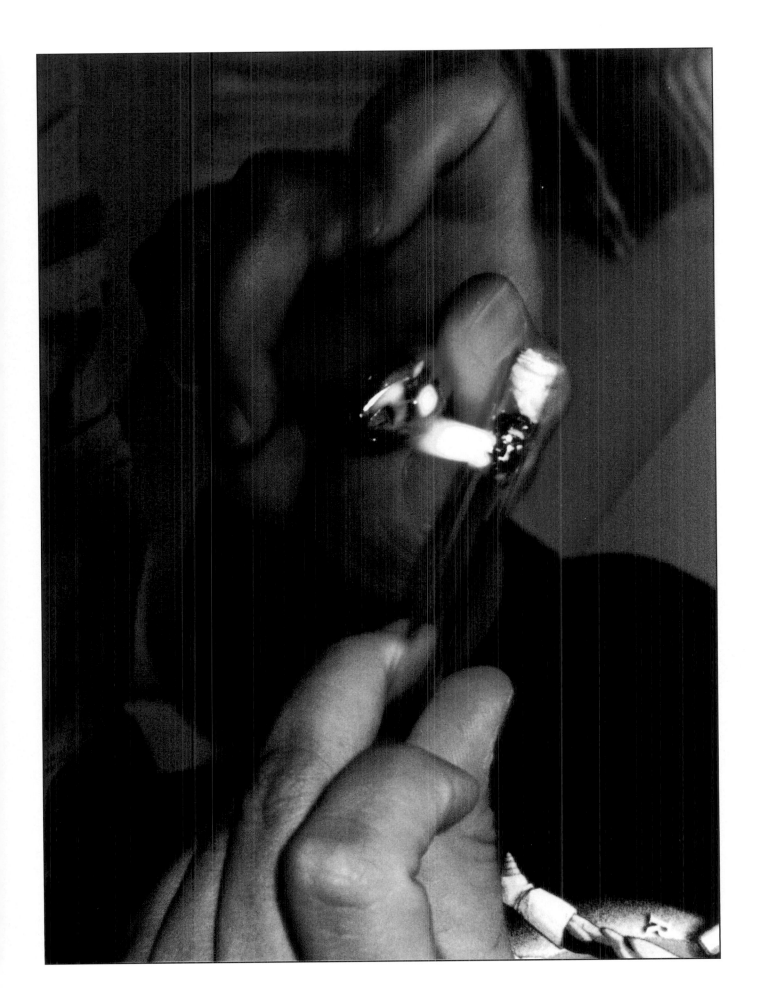

Heroin

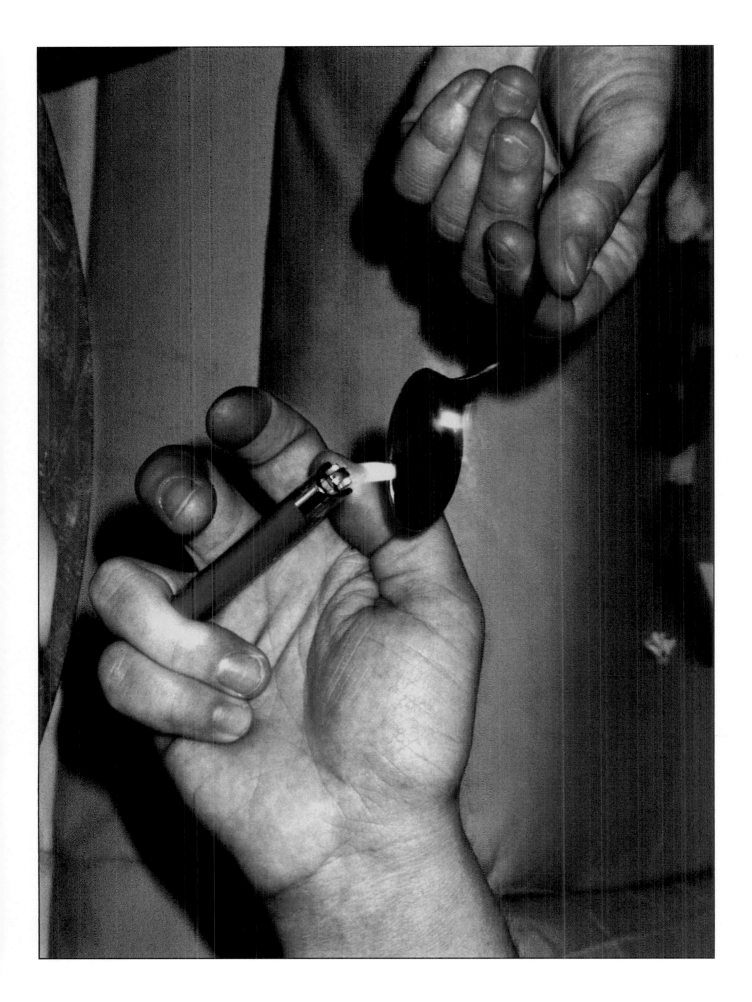

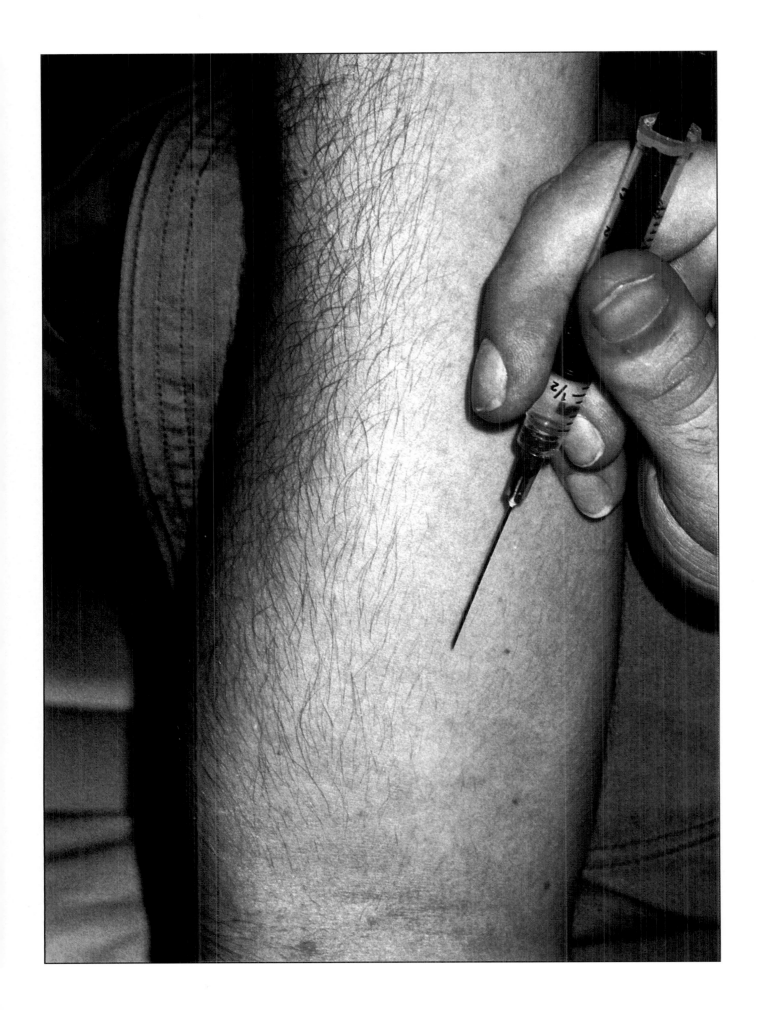

Marijuana

Conventional Treatment

Conventional substance abuse treatment programs advocate the total avoidance of these triggers. Self-help groups such as Alcoholics Anonymous and Narcotics Anonymous instruct their members to stay away from the people, places, and things associated with their substance abusing past. Treatment programs also recognize the power of these conditioned associations and strongly advise total avoidance of the triggers. Although this is excellent advice, it isn't always practical advice. Some exposure is inevitable. When exposure does occur the conventional advice is to call one's sponsor or other support person to enlist her help with not giving into temptation.

On the surface, it would seem reasonable to advise people who are addicted to drugs and alcohol to avoid triggers that set off their desire to use. But there are two problems with this approach: the practical and the theoretical.

First, in effect it becomes very limiting and often impossible to avoid all triggers without isolating someone from the world. Although you can avoid the old circle of friends and hangouts, replace them with a new clique of friends and new places to mingle, it is virtually impossible to avoid all exposure to addictive substances and their cues.

Second, theoretically speaking, avoidance of stimuli does not result in the elimination of the conditioned response. Consider the following example. An addict has devoted years to avoiding the sight and smell of the drug as well as the people, places, and things associated with it. Predictably, if and when she faces the triggers, she will have the same reaction as she did years ago. This will lead her to be discouraged because of her lack of progress. Her reaction may also frighten her. It will also reinforce the mind-set, "once an addict, always an addict." If she does not give in to the temptation, she will probably redouble her efforts to avoid these triggers. For this reason self-help groups wisely urge their members to attend meetings for the rest of their lives, to always be ready and prepared for obstacles, and to believe they will always be an addict no matter how long they remain clean.

An Alternative and Complementary Approach

ERP therapy is an alternative and complementary solution to this problem. It's a way to raise a person's ability to control his impulse to use and thereby protect him when he is exposed to conditioned stimuli. The ERP therapy concept is very straightforward: If a person is exposed to his trigger but does not consume the drug or alcohol, his response to it will eventually extinguish. Psychologists call this process of exposure without taking action an *extinction curve.*

As ERP therapy takes hold, the person will not feel the urge to use in the presence of the triggers and will feel comfortable enough and safe enough not to use if and when he is accidentally exposed to a former trigger.

For example, a person who always used marijuana while listening to a particular song will probably have the urge to smoke pot whenever the song is played. Rather than avoiding the song all together, listening to the song over and over again without the use of marijuana will eventually decrease the intensity of the impulse. The most important aspect is to set up the scenario so the person cannot use while the song is playing. This is called "response prevention."

In the above example, ERP weakens the connection between using and certain associated stimuli (such as a song). ERP can also be used, however, to reduce the impulses to use triggered by sight, smell, and feel of drugs and alcohol themselves. If you deliberately expose yourself to sight, smell, and feel of drugs and alcohol, but do not use them, eventually the harmful substances will no longer be as attractive.

A second part of the relapse puzzle involves what is called *operant conditioning*. Operant conditioning refers to the positive and negative reinforcement you receive from using an addictive substance. Positive reinforcement is something "good" you gain as result of performing a set of actions. A paycheck is one of the primary positive reinforcements we receive by working. Negative reinforcement is something "bad" that is eliminated or reduced as a result of performing a set of actions. Giving into the strident demands of a tantruming child is negatively reinforcing to a parent (in the short run) because it ends the child's tantrum. Many people confuse punishment with negative reinforcement. They are not the same. Punishment occurs when a "bad" thing happens as a result of a set of actions. Getting a $300 speeding ticket is a common example of punishment. If you can talk a policeman out of giving you that ticket that result is negative reinforcement (because you eliminated the $300 fine).

This brings us back to addictive behavior. Most addicts find it difficult to resist using long enough to discover that the impulse often subsides in a few minutes. Instead, the more common behavior is to give in, to obtain the positive and negative reinforcement associated with the addictive substance. If, however, the impulse is allowed time to pass, the operant behavior (using drugs and/or alcohol) does not occur. Successfully resisting the impulse to use does two things. First, it weakens the impulse. Second, the lack of negative reinforcement (that is, the elimination of the uncomfortable cravings) and the lack of positive reinforcement (the gaining of pleasure, social togetherness, etc.) for drug-using behavior will weaken the future strength of that behavior. This process is called *operant extinction*. Once you are able to crave and not use drugs or alcohol, your new ability to cope with your cravings in a healthy way will be positively reinforced by successful abstinence, the joy of loved ones, and increased self-esteem.

New Coping Behavior

The final part of the relapse puzzle involves learning new coping behaviors. You can replace old addictive behaviors that were triggered by stimuli previously associated with drug and alcohol use with your new coping behaviors. This reconditioning process will help you to react in new and healthy ways to triggers that previously made you crave and then use.

This reconditioning can be achieved in the following way. Besides solely exposing the addicted person to simulated drugs or alcohol and waiting for the impulse to subside, the person can focus his energy on thoughts that will be helpful to remember if he is placed in a situation where real drugs or alcohol are present. Although most addicts know the risks they are taking, as well as the frightening consequences, these thoughts do not make it to the forefronts of their minds when it matters most. When faced with a drinking or drugging situation, most addicts think, " I want it, I want it, I want it." This is their dysfunctional cognitive script. The thoughts of health risks, physical damage to themselves, and difficulties with peers, families, and employers do not enter the picture. Instead they generate cognitive statements such as "I don't care," or "That will not happen to me," or "I'll deal with that when and if it occurs."

To counter these minimizing responses, the person needs to be trained to generate more suitable cognitive scripts, such as "I want to keep my job," "I want to feel good about myself," or "This unpleasant feeling will pass," to use when exposed to substance using stimuli. Armed with a functional arsenal of statements, the addicted person can focus on them by reading them, repeating them, and by hearing them being read. In this way, the sights and smells as well as any other conditioned stimuli associated with substance abuse will trigger these new more adaptive thoughts rather than the old minimizing thoughts. During ERP therapy, the new cognitive scripts are also associated with a relaxation response to further increase their effectiveness.

ERP can help a substance abusing person once she has made a commitment to changing her behavior. ERP works by extinguishing the addictive behavior triggered by stimuli associated with drug and alcohol use. ERP also teaches you new coping skills that you can use to replace your old addictive behavior. In this way, cravings triggered by future exposure will be minimal, and your new coping skills will be triggered instead. The ultimate goal of ERP therapy is to replace your self-destructive cycle with a virtuous cycle that rewards non-use with increases in self-esteem and self-efficacy.

The next chapter explains how to conduct your own ERP sessions. It will carefully and simply explain each step of the reconditioning process, what to expect as you do ERP, and what precautions you need to take.

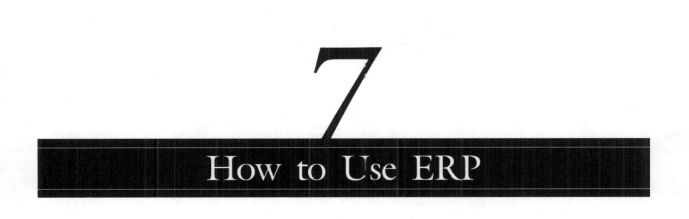

7

How to Use ERP

We'll begin this chapter by providing detailed instructions for each step of an ERP photo card session, including: monitoring your craving level, deep breathing, taking your pulse, body scanning, and creating cognitive script cards. Then we will walk through the nuts and bolts of conducting the actual session. First, however, you must make sure that self-directed ERP is appropriate for you.

Who Should Use Self-Directed ERP?

If you have not already done so now is the time to take the Addiction Intensity Scale (AIS) test. You can find the AIS in the Introduction. If your AIS score is in the moderate or severe level of addiction intensity, then you can proceed with photo card ERP on a self-help basis. If you scored at the catastrophic AIS level then, before proceeding, you will need to enter an intensive outpatient treatment program (you may also require some time in a residential treatment program). We recommend that you enter the intensive outpatient program prior to using ERP.

   If your AIS score is at the terminal level of intensity then you will definitely need a residential treatment program, and you should not attempt ERP until you have safely entered one. ERP will not be helpful to you without the safety and intensive treatment that a residential program provides. Please follow our advice in this regard to the letter.

The Craving Wave

The "Craving Wave" explains how people respond to substance use triggers and cues—both internal and external ones. Your objective is to learn to *believe* that you can "ride the wave" and not let yourself be triggered to use drugs or alcohol.

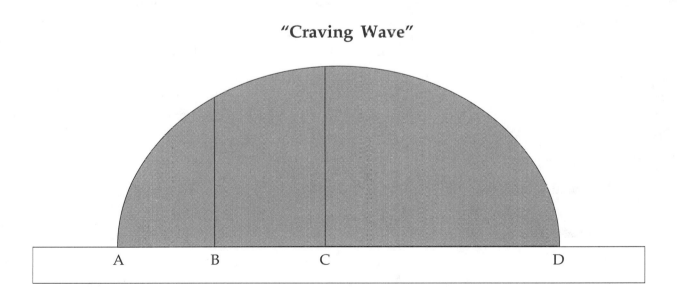

"Craving Wave"

An impulse to use begins at point A, when you have been exposed to an external stimulus formerly associated with substance use or to thoughts and memories of using. Once an impulse is initiated, it will increase in strength as illustrated at point B. When people in recovery get to point B on the Craving Wave, they start to feel very uncomfortable. In street talk, they are starting to "jones." Their drug using history has conditioned them to alleviate these feelings by using their substance of choice. When you get to point C, your desire to use will be at its strongest. But it will not remain at that level of intensity. If you do not use, you will discover something very empowering: at point D your impulse to use will have faded away.

In an ERP session, you will prove to yourself that you can reach point C, feel uncomfortable, and NOT use. Once you are able to do this, you will feel a tremendous sense of empowerment. You will know that you have the power to ignore your cravings, and that by doing so, they will fade away.

After completing thirty ERP sessions, you will know for certain that you can ride your Craving Wave without using the substance. In short, you will become a believer. The more ERP sessions you do, the more you will reinforce your new and very empowering skills. Ride the Craving Wave to success!

Deep Breathing and Pulse-Taking Directions

Your next step is to learn deep breathing techniques so you can relax yourself at will. We will also explain how to take your pulse. Your pulse is a good indicator of your general level of excitation/relaxation.

Deep Breathing

First you are going to learn a way to breathe that will help you to relax. This is a special kind of breathing, similar to the type of breathing taught at a yoga or meditation class. This kind of deep breathing involves breathing *in* through your nose and *out* through your mouth, pausing in between each inhalation and exhalation. One cycle of breathing = inhale + pause + exhale.

1. Sit in a symmetrical position. Rest your hands on your thighs, with your palms down.

2. Inhale to a count of five. To keep count, lightly tap your fingers in sequence on your knee, starting with your right pinky. Taps should be about one second apart.

3. Pause for a count of ten. Hold your breath during this count, and close both hands into light fists.

4. Exhale to a count of five. Use your fingers to count, this time with your left hand.

5. Practice doing this as rhythmically as possible until you are good at it. It will take several practice sessions before you get the coordination right. Be patient with yourself.

6. After you have mastered the technique, you are ready to expand the inhale/exhale count. Gradually increase your count for inhaling from 5 to 10, continue to pause for

a count of 10, and increase your exhale count to 10. Most people will find it easier to exhale to a count of 10 than to inhale to the same count. If you are a smoker you may not be able to reach 10. In this case get as far above five as you can.

How to Take Your Pulse

To take your pulse, place your right hand palm side up. Using the index and middle fingers of your left hand, place them on your radial bone (which is below the thumb area and at the start of the wrist), slowly slide your fingers toward the center of your wrist until you find the pulse. Once you have found your pulse, get a watch that counts seconds. Time your pulse for 15 seconds and count the number of beats. Then convert this number into beats per minute by consulting the following chart or multiplying the number of beats you counted in 15 seconds by four.

Beats Counted in 15 Seconds	Beats per Minute
15	60
16	64
17	68
18	72
19	76
20	80
21	84
22	88
23	92
24	96
25	100
26	104
27	108
28	112
29	116
30	120

Body Scan Directions

Once you are able to complete ten cycles of inhale/pause/exhale and have learned to take your pulse, you will be ready to learn body scanning. Body scanning is an easy technique to help you to identify sources of stress and anxiety in your body.

1. Sit in a chair (preferably one without arms) using good posture.

2. Remain in a relaxed position—symmetrical, legs uncrossed, feet flat on the floor. Let your arms rest in your lap. If you rest your arms on the arms of the chair your shoulders will tend to go up.

3. You're going to do a body scan, so that you can pinpoint where and when your muscles are tense. Close your eyes and concentrate on your feet. Are they tense? Are your toes curled up inside your shoe? If your toes are curled up or tense, wiggle them around and let them relax.

4. Now move up to your shins. Make sure they're relaxed.

5. Now your knees. Are you holding them together tightly? If so, let them drop apart naturally.

6. Now your thighs and buttocks. Are you holding them tightly? If so, release them and feel yourself sink deeply into the chair.

7. Move up to your stomach. Are you holding tensions there? Is your waistband or belt too tight? If so, loosen it.

8. Now turn your attention to your hands. Are you clenching your fists? If so, shake out your hands and let them flop back into your lap.

9. Move your attention to your shoulders. Are you holding them up? If so, wiggle them around and let them drop.

10. Now concentrate on the feelings in your jaw. Are you clenching your teeth? Are you pressing your lips tightly shut? If so, let them go. Let your jaw drop.

11. Now your eyes and forehead. Are you squeezing your eyes shut? Are you making wrinkles on your forehead? If so, let them go. Make your forehead smooth.

12. Now take one last moment to make sure your entire body is relaxed and comfortable. If you want to shift around a bit to get more comfortable, do so.

13. You've now completed a body scan. You can do this anytime and anyplace quickly and without being noticed. If you can pinpoint where you're holding tension, you make yourself feel more relaxed. If you don't even know you're tense, then you'll just stay tense.

14. You may want to record these instructions on an audiotape and play them when doing your body scan. You can also order a body scan tape from SLS Health by calling 1-888-CARE-4U.

Your Cognitive Script Cards

Cognitive scripts are alternative thought patterns you want to associate with craving triggers to help you to say no to your cravings. From the list below, select ten cognitive scripts that you think will be effective for you. Write each one on a 3-by-5-inch index card using a black Magic Marker. Make sure the script fills the entire card and is easy to read. You will use these cards in your ERP sessions. The suggestions below were the ones our patients came up with in the course of their ERP treatment. Of course, we encourage you to develop your own cognitive scripts. The following may help to stimulate your creativity.

- I want and deserve a good future for myself.

- Remember how lousy it was the last time I got high (or drunk).

- I will regain my self-respect and dignity if I walk away.

- Remember the high-risk situations I faced while drunk or high.

- I will be a positive role model for my children if I walk away.

- I will be a positive role model for my family if I walk away.

- I will be a positive role model for my friends if I walk away.

- Remember the times I stole to get my drugs.

- I will be able to hold down and maintain a job if I walk away.

- My hopes and dreams for the future will come true if I walk away.

- I am a good person and don't need to prove that by using.

- I will be able to get in touch with my true feelings if I walk away.

- My family will be proud of me if I walk away.

- I will be proud of myself if I walk away.

- Remember the pain and hurt I caused my family and myself.

- Remember the time(s) I almost died due to my drug use.

- I don't want to end up like my father.

- I will reduce my chances of going to rehab if I walk away.

- I will reduce my chances of going to jail if I walk away.

- I will get off probation sooner if I walk away.

- Remember the time(s) I spent in jail.

- I will be able to feel better about myself if I walk away.

- Remember the time(s) I prostituted myself to get drugs.

- Remember my mother's look on her face when she found me on the street.

- If I walk away my physical health will improve.

- If I continue to use I will lose everything.

- Remember how my tic disorder was affected by my using.

- I will be stronger and more in control if I walk away.

- Remember the time(s) I acted like a fool in front of my boss.

- If I walk away I can retain my possessions.

- Remember how I drove home and don't remember getting there.
- I will decrease my chances of overdosing if I walk away.
- Remember the feeling while I was coming down off the high.
- Remember the physical pain and consequences of withdrawal.
- I will be able to open up my own business if I walk away.
- My hopes of having a wife and child will come true if I walk away.
- I will reduce the chances of killing myself if I walk away.
- I will be able to communicate better if I walk away.
- Remember how angry my family became when I drank.
- I am a worthwhile and productive person.
- My sexually promiscuous behaviors will decrease if I walk away.
- Remember losing everything I owned because of the drugs.
- I will be able to spend money on healthy alternatives if I walk away.
- Remember how paranoid I became when I used.
- Remember the stupid things I did to get my drugs.
- I will be able to get my children back if I walk away.
- I will live a more independent and worthwhile life if I walk away.
- I will live a calmer and more peaceful life if I walk away.
- If I continue to use I will *die*.

You can select more than ten cognitive scripts if you like. Be sure to select ones (or write ones of your own) that have a strong emotional impact for you. Emotionally weak scripts are ineffective conditioning stimuli.

Preparing for Your First ERP Session

1. Review the theory and rationale behind ERP found in chapter 6. Pay particular attention to the idea that your cravings will gradually fade away. When you reach this point, the sight of your former addictive substance will no longer trigger an impulse to use.

2. Remember that the cognitive scripts on the cards gradually become associated to the sight of the drug/alcohol until they pop into your mind automatically. They will come to replace the idea that now pops into your mind automatically: i.e., "Gimme."

3. Recall from chapter 4 how the rationale of ERP is different from that of other treatments, which emphasize avoiding "people, places, and things." Recall, too, why this traditional strategy is not always practical.

4. Keep in mind the details of what will happen emotionally during the ERP session.

   - Make sure you or your ERP buddy stops the session if the situation becomes dangerously stimulating for you.

   - Keep in mind that the photographs of drugs or alcohol will stimulate urges or cravings to use. Even though you know the drugs are "pretend," you will have the same emotional reaction. For example, you cry at a sad movie or feel tense at a horror film, even though you know it is not real. In these "fantasy" situations, the emotional part of the brain does not know the difference between pretend and reality.

   - Some things to expect during the ERP session, immediately after and in the long run from ERP: anxiety, cravings, the passing of your cravings and anxiety, a lessening or elimination of your cravings when you are around triggers, and finally, an ability to "just say no."

5. Review the "Craving Wave" section on page 73. It describes how to "ride the Craving Wave" without using and what to expect.

6. Most importantly, be prepared to use your support network (AA, NA, friend, therapist, loved one, etc.). Make sure you have the necessary resources to get through the ERP session, as well as the potentially difficult time after each session. Talk to someone after each session, and use your relaxation activities, meetings, etc., to reduce your craving levels.

7. Generate ten to fifteen personalized cognitive scripts for your ERP session. See page 77 for cognitive script suggestions.

8. Study the "Here and Now Craving Scales." These scales can be found in Appendix A, page 127.

9. Be sure to practice and complete one cycle of the deep breathing and body scanning techniques described on pages 74–76.

ERP Online

You can also do ERP online at *www.killthecraving.com*. Our Web site will guide you through as many ERP sessions as you need to help you get control of you impulse to use drugs and alcohol. You will find helpful recovery tips and our advisory service, the E-Mail Counselor, there. The E-Mail Counselor allows you to get advice and support by e-mail to help make your recovery a successful one. Just click your way to *www.killthecraving.com* and use "bookreader" as your user name and the last five digits of this book's ISBN number as your password.

How to Run a Photo Card ERP Session

You are now ready to do an ERP session. You will use your deep breathing and body scanning skills during ERP, so make sure that you have practiced them. You are not ready for ERP if you cannot use deep breathing to relax yourself so that you feel completely calm.

Precautions to Take

You need to decide whether to conduct your session alone or with a buddy. If you would feel safer with assistance, ask a friend to help you out. Instruct him or her to help make sure you do not raise your craving level so high that you want to go out and get high.

If at any time during your ERP session you get nervous, overwhelmed, scared, or experience intense cravings, immediately *stop* and complete a deep breathing and body scan.

Materials You Will Need

- ERP photo cards (marijuana, heroin, cocaine, crack, alcohol) found in the photo insert in the center of the book. Each set of cards contains four pictures except the alcohol set which contains three cards.

- Here and Now Craving (HNC) Scales, page 127

- Deep breathing and body scan instructions, pages 74 and 75

- Your cognitive scripts (at least ten), see pages 76–78

- Music of choice (that you associate with getting high or drunk)

- ERP session form, see page 81

ERP Session Form

Date of Session _____ Session Number _____

ERP Card Set Used: □ Marijuana   □ Crack   □ Cocaine   □ Heroin   □ Alcohol

Session Measurement	Craving Level (0 to 10). Use the HNC scales for reference points	Pulse Rate (BPM)	Did you complete this card? Any comments?
Baseline			
After Card 1			
After Card 2			
After Card 3			
After Card 4			

Session Notes:

Instructions (See also Visual Instructions starting on page 84)

1. Gather all necessary items needed for the ERP session as noted above.

2. Find a comfortable place to sit where you will not be disturbed for at least twenty minutes. Turn the telephone off.

3. Take a baseline reading of your craving level and your pulse rate. Write these down on your ERP session form (see page 81). Make as many copies of this form as you would like.

4. Ask yourself:
   "Am I ready to focus on ERP and put away whatever else is on my mind for now?"
   If you are ready, then proceed.
   If you are not ready, stay focused on the relaxation techniques until you are. Say to yourself:
   "It may be hard for me to concentrate because I'm feeling this way but I can do this."
   If you cannot get yourself focused on doing your session now then postpone the session.

5. Briefly review the rationale behind ERP by asking yourself,
   "Why am I doing ERP?"
   Correct answers include the following:

   - "So I won't get a craving when I see or smell drugs and alcohol. After ERP I'll have about as much reaction to them as I have to seeing a couch." (Extinction curve)

   - "So I think of or remember the cognitive scripts when I see or smell the drugs or alcohol." (Acquiring a new conditioned response)

   - "So I will be able to remain in recovery and not use again."

6. Start one complete cycle of relaxation. Start ten cycles of deep breathing. What is your maximum count for inhaling comfortably? For exhaling? Next perform a body scan. (See deep breathing and body scan instructions on pages 74 and 75).

7. Put on music that you associate with your drug or alcohol use. Play the music softly but audibly.

8. Take out the photo cards of your drug of choice (alcohol, cocaine, crack, heroin, or marijuana).

9. Look at the first ERP photo card for about thirty seconds. Study it carefully. Remember how it felt. Your cravings will be stirred up by thinking of the following:

   - "I really want to take a hit (drink) of this."

   - "Wouldn't this taste good right now?"

   - "This will make me feel great."

   - "I want to get high, don't I?"

   - "This would relieve me of all my stress and make me forget about all of my problems."

10. Read aloud each cognitive script card. Associate each script with your target substance and the cravings it creates in you. (Your cards should be printed in thick, black Magic Marker and cover the entire face of the index card).

11. When you have completed the first pass through the cognitive scripts, take out the Here and Now Craving Scales (pages 127–30). Ask yourself, "How much do I want this?" Use the scales to decide your craving level, which can range from 0 to 10: "0" is "not at all" and "10" is "I want it so badly that I'd grab it right now if I could." What is your craving level? (It should be higher than when you started your ERP session.) Write your craving number on your ERP session form. Next, take your pulse and record it on the ERP session form.

12. If your body language, craving rating, or thinking shows that you are getting extremely agitated or anxious, put the ERP photo cards away for now. Complete a cycle of deep breathing and body scanning. It's okay to feel like you want to use. The feeling will pass. Stay with the procedure and you will find out that this is exactly what will happen. Think about the Craving Wave. Desire increases rapidly, peaks out, and then declines almost as rapidly. Ride the wave until it is gone.

13. Proceed to the next card and repeat steps 9 to 12. When you have finished the second card, go on to the next one. Stop your session when you have gone through all the cards *or* when you reach a point where your craving level is too high for you to safely continue. *Do not* be shy about stopping your session if the craving gets too strong. Remember, ERP means exposure and response prevention. ERP will not work if it triggers you to use.

Closing the Session

1. When you have reached the end of the photo card exposure, put away the ERP photo cards. Close with ten cycles of deep breathing and a body scan. Then rate your final craving level on the 0 to 10 point scale and record this number. Finally, take your pulse and record this number as well.

2. Close your eyes for one minute and evaluate the progress you have made. How many cards were you able to view? How high did your craving level go? Ask yourself, "What will I do when I leave this session if I experience a craving?" Answer: Remember your cards, talk to someone, call someone, exercise, or do some deep breathing. And most of all *wait* before acting on your impulse to use. Ride the wave until it is gone!

3. End the session by focusing all of your psychological energy on the following passage. Try to visualize what these words mean:
"Remember, when I see my drug of choice out there in the real world, I'll have less of an urge, and I'll think of what was on the cards. If these two things happen, I'll be less likely to use."

4. Enjoy a healthy activity after you have completed your session—a workout, conversation with a good friend, movie, dinner out, or a similar activity.

ERP Visual Instructions

Following is a set the visual instructions for running an ERP session.

1. Take your baseline pulse, rate your craving level, and record them on the ERP session form. (Follow instructions on how to take your pulse from page 75. For craving level, refer to the Here and Now Craving Scales on pages 129 and 130.)

2. Complete ten full cycles of deep breathing. (Follow instructions from page 74.)

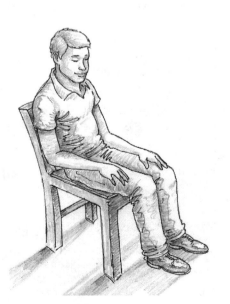

3. Complete one body scan cycle. (Follow instructions from pages 75–76.)

4. Take out the ERP photo cards and look at the first card for about thirty seconds. Read aloud each cognitive script. Associate each statement with the drug in the photo and make note of any cravings.

5. When you have completed the first card, take out the ERP session form and record your craving level and pulse rate. (For craving level, refer to the Here and Now Craving Scales on pages 129 to 130).

6. Proceed to the next card and repeat steps four and five. Try to get through the entire series of ERP photo cards.

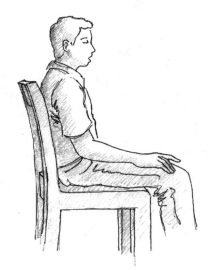

7. Complete ten full cycles of deep breathing. (Follow instructions from page 74).

8. Complete one body scan cycle. (Follow instructions from pages 75–76).

9. Take your pulse, rate your final craving level, and record them on the ERP session form. (Follow instructions on how to take your pulse from page 75. For craving level, refer to the Here and Now Craving Scales on pages 129 and 130).

10. Each ERP session finishes with a healthy and enjoyable recreational activity. Be sure to schedule one such activity after each of your ERP sessions. This is a critical part of your ERP therapy.

Thirty Full Sessions Is Your Goal

Your final therapy goal is to complete thirty ERP sessions in which you are able to view all the ERP cards for your target substance, with a final session rating of less than 3 and a pulse rate within 5 beats per minute of your first session's initial baseline. If you are not able to go through all the cards in a session because you became overstimulated, don't feel disappointed. This means that ERP is working for you and that you will need several sessions to get through all the cards. Once you reach this first goal, you can then work toward the final goal of thirty full sessions. Remember, you must push yourself to complete thirty full sessions even if you think you don't need it—you really do.

Tracking Your Progress

To help you keep track of your progress, we have two tracking forms you can use. The first form tracks goal number one (view all the cards in an ERP photo set). The second tracks the second goal (run thirty ERP sessions).

Goal One

The first goal is to view all cards in your target substance's ERP photo card set in a single session. Next to each corresponding card number under the session column, record whether you were able to view the card during the session.

Card Number for set: _____	Session Date	Session Date	Session Date	Session Date
1				
2				
3				
4				

Goal Two

The second goal is to run thirty full ERP sessions with final craving rating of less than 3 and a pulse rate within 5 beats per minute of your first session's initial baseline. Record the session date of each session in which you viewed all of the target substance ERP photos and record your final craving rating and pulse rate from the session's end.

Session Date	Final Pulse Rate	Final Craving Rating	Session Date	Final Pulse Rate	Final Craving Rating
1			9		
2			10		
3			11		
4			12		
5			13		
6			14		
7			15		
8			16		

Session Date	Final Pulse Rate	Final Craving Rating	Session Date	Final Pulse Rate	Final Craving Rating
17			24		
18			25		
19			26		
20			27		
21			28		
22			29		
23			30		

Points to Remember

1. ERP is not, by itself, a cure for your addiction. ERP is a more effective treatment tool if it is used in conjunction with a recovery support group (a 12-step group or another kind) and some form of psychotherapy (individual or group). All of these components can make ERP a more productive way to reduce your cravings to use drugs or alcohol.

2. At first, your craving levels may be high, due to the anticipatory anxiety you may encounter from these sessions. However, as you become more familiar with the rationale, process, and cards, and particularly after you gain self-confidence with beating the addiction, your body will become less reactive to the stimuli.

3. If, during the ERP session, you become overwhelmed or anxious, *stop immediately*. Put all of the ERP photo cards away and begin to complete the relaxation exercises written in the book. Feel free to add other relaxation techniques that may work to reduce your stress and anxieties. If necessary, call a friend for support.

4. If you experience cravings or anxiety after your ERP session, remember that you are in control over the addiction. Keep yourself busy (ride out the Craving Wave), by going to a meeting, exercising, talking to someone, going for a walk, going somewhere safe, writing in a journal, listening to music (*not* the music associated with substance use that you use during your ERP session), reciting your cognitive scripts, or calling your therapist.

5. After thirty sessions of ERP, if you still are experiencing craving levels in excess of 3 on the Here and Now Craving Scales, you should do another block of five sessions.

People vary in the number of sessions required to reduce their craving levels below 3. Continue to run ERP sessions until you are able to do so.

6. ERP can also be done with a therapist. You can get more information about this option by calling us at 1-888-8-CARE-4U.

8

Reclaiming Your Lifestyle

You've made the commitment to recovery, you've built your support network, and you've started to kill your cravings. You've reduced or eliminated your substance use. You are now ready to repair the damage your addiction has done to your life. You are ready to redesign your lifestyle to support a healthier way of living.

The key to the successful management of an addiction-free lifestyle is balance. Your objective is to achieve the proper balance of work, play, love, self-care, and recovery support. You must guard against getting caught up in a rat race of recovery support activities to the exclusion of everything else. You need to find activities that can fill the void left by your addictive routines. That is, you must learn how to have fun without drugs and alcohol. For some people this is one of the biggest challenges.

You can reclaim your lifestyle if you invest a little bit of time in planning the changes and enhancements you would like to make. We will walk you through this planning process to make it as easy as possible for you.

Repair List

Step one is to make a list of the damage done to your life by your former addictions. This list should include financial damage, relationship damage, health damage, career damage, license loss, and housing problems. We have developed a checklist to help you identify specific repairs that need to be done.

Your Lifestyle Repair List

Problem	Yes	Repair Solution and Target Date	X
I lost my driver's license			
I have credit card debt I cannot pay			
My credit rating is poor			
I have been evicted from my apartment			
I need dental work			
I get sick frequently			
My professional license has been suspended			
My parents do not trust me			
My lover does not trust me			

Problem	Yes	Repair Solution and Target Date	X
I am unemployed			
My resume has gaps in it			
I have unpaid traffic tickets			
I have DWI conviction(s)			
I have possession conviction(s)			
I have pending criminal charges			
I am on probation			
I have bills I cannot pay			
I do not have a checking account			
I do not have a credit card			
I have financial liens against my wages			
I need to change my career or line of work			
I need a new place to live			
I need new friends; my old ones are addicts			

To complete your repair list, place a check in the "Yes" column for each item that applies to you. Add any additional items that you do not find listed in the blank spaces on the bottom of the form.

The next step is to think of how you would go about repairing the problem. Jot down your ideas in the "Repair Solution" column. For example, if you lost your driver's license, your repair solution might be to get the number of the motor vehicle department in your area, call them, and find out what steps you have to take to get your license back (e.g., pay back tickets, complete a safe-driving course, fill out an application, and pay a fee). Once you have gathered all the repair information that you need for an item, you can set its implementation target date. The target date should give you enough time to complete all the steps and repair the problem as best as you can (in our example, the solution would be to get your driver's license back). When you have implemented your solution, mark the item off in the "X" column.

Another repair problem example might be to make amends with a family member or close friend from whom you stole money to get drugs. This is a tougher problem to handle than getting your license back, because of the intense emotions that are involved (we offered suggestions for how to go about this in Chapter 5). In the solution section of your repair list, make notes about when and where you would talk with the person. You might also want to create a point-by-point outline of what you would like to say. Finally, once you figure out how long it will take you to summon the courage to approach the person, you could set a target date for implementing this solution.

Once you have completed your repair list, you need to look it over. Which item are you going to tackle first? After you have decided, implement its solution before going back to the list to work on the next item. Tackle one problem at a time: fix it or pass it by and select another. Do not spend a lot of time thinking about repairing an item. Do it or skip it and then select another.

Procrastination is your enemy! It is only natural to avoid doing unpleasant things, but the longer you avoid them, the longer your life will remain damaged—and the longer your emotions will be all twisted and painful. Besides, it is a tremendous relief to repair something your addiction screwed up. Remember this: A repaired lifestyle is a happier lifestyle. Just do it.

New and Improved Lifestyle

Dreams, enjoyment, discovery, respect, love, accomplishment, savings, and self-esteem are among the many things you can have now that you are recovering from addiction. Recovery isn't as much about giving something up as it is about discovering what you really want from life—your life.

Take a moment to recall someone you knew who died. Would he or she have preferred to be young and alive today? What happens when someone dies? Does her soul survive or does she cease to exist along with her body? Is life to be taken for granted? Or is it to be cherished and valued every moment of each day? One day, death will come for you. How will you feel on that day? Will you want more time or will you welcome death? When you look back on your life will you feel good about the life you lived? Or will you feel that you cheated yourself and wasted your days foolishly? These are very important questions because they go to the heart of why it is so important to reorganize your lifestyle around the things and people that truly matter to you. Life is short—much shorter than any of us realize! So there is precious little time left to waste. It is time to discover what it is you really want from your life.

The first thing we hope you want is to remain in recovery. You want to overcome your addiction once and for all. You want to repair the damage that you have done to your lifestyle. Beyond these two things there are many other desires and aspirations that have been pushed aside by your addiction. How do you get in touch with these things? Here are some questions that can help you unlock your hidden (and not so hidden) desires.

When you were a young kid, maybe eight or nine, what kind of creative games did you enjoy playing? Did you ever make up a game of your own? If so, what was it?

When you graduated high school, what did you want to do with your life more than anything else? Forget the practical, what was your most exciting dream? Did you want to travel? Did you want to enter a line of work everyone told you to avoid? Did you have a hobby or sports interest that you spent many hours of time on? Did you enjoy baseball or dancing? Were you pretty good at drawing or painting? Did you enjoy building things or cooking? Did you enjoy collecting things such as glassware, stamps, baseball cards, or toys? Is there a musical instrument that you always wanted to learn to play? Or how about a sport you always wanted to take up? Are you getting the idea? You can fill the void created by past addiction with the things you've always wanted to do but have forgotten. We all have many untapped interests and desires that we've ignored or put aside. One of the reasons you put these interests aside is that you think negatively about them. You tell yourself (often because others have told you first) that you have no talent or ability for it, or worse yet, that you won't really like it if you try it. Perhaps you even say to yourself that you'd look like a fool if you tried to learn this or that. Or that it will take too much time or money to get good at it. It's just not worth it. But none of this is true. They are mere excuses for not taking a chance—a chance to get into something you may truly enjoy!

Now is the time to rethink past reasons for not developing an interest or desire. Now is the time that you need something new and healthy to focus your energy and time on. Now is the time to express yourself in exciting, new, and self-fulfilling ways. The void created by your past addiction needs to be filled with things that you love doing—not just work and daily routines. Going to work, paying bills, feeding yourself, cleaning the house, and doing errands are important parts of everyone's life but they do not give life the meaning and purpose it needs to give you special joy. In fact, one of the biggest recovery mistakes people make is getting trapped in a cycle of work, pay bills, eat, go to meetings, stay home, and sleep. After a while it becomes boring and depressing, and once it does, it becomes a powerful relapse trigger: "I just need some fun in my life. One time won't hurt." To guard against this happening to you, you need to develop healthy activities that you can enjoy for the pure pleasure of just doing them.

One twenty-something-year-old man (addicted since his early teens) discovered baseball. Baseball had been an interest of his when he was a young child. He remembered how much he loved pitching in his Little League games. So he decided to join a softball league during his first summer of recovery. This led to the discovery of golf. He started to play golf and enjoyed it so much that it has become a new, much healthier "addiction."

Trial and error is part of discovering new passions and interests. Try something you think you might enjoy, then see if you do. If you don't, try something else—don't be discouraged. Risk taking is the part of being addicted that you can put to good use now that you are in recovery. Addicted people frequently take big risks to satisfy their addictive cravings. Now that you are out of that game, you can still take risks—healthy ones—by trying different activities until you find something you really like. Trying different things is also part of the fun of discovering what you really want from your life.

To further help you along, we have provided a list of special interest magazines on our *www.killthecraving.com* Web site that cover activities from dirt bike riding to coin collecting. These magazines will help you get familiar with an activity so you can decide whether to pursue it. You can buy a copy of one of these magazines or browse them at a local newsstand or bookstore. You can also get a wealth of information about an interest on the Internet by typing the interest's description into a search engine such as Yahoo or Excite. You'll find hundreds of links that will help you explore your potential interest in greater depth.

Time Management

You are always late: for appointments, picking up the kids, turning in schoolwork, paying bills, and sometimes even your job. Your credibility is "flat-lined." The passage of time is easily ignored. If you have a car, you've probably received a few speeding tickets because you are late. If you rely on public transportation, "the bus was late" is no longer an acceptable excuse—even if the bus *is* late. It's your problem, so you must learn to manage your time carefully. Good time-management skills are essential to maintaining your recovery and repairing your life.

Plan Your Time

Unplanned, dead time is toxic to your recovery. Remember what you used to do with your spare time? Most likely, that "downtime" was when the impulse to use was at its strongest. Getting back into an addiction-free lifestyle necessitates self-discipline, repetitiveness, and flexibility. Tight time management will improve your reliability and help repair your reputation. To manage your time effectively, 7 days, 168 total hours, need to be planned. Typically these hours are allocated as followed.

- 40–60 hours working

- 40–60 hours sleeping

- 8–10 hours self-care, eating

- 5–10 hours commuting

- 3–5 hours house/clothes cleaning

As you can see, that leaves a minimum 23 hours remaining in a week for scheduling activities that can enhance your lifestyle in a healthy, productive manner. When you plan, wellness, personal satisfaction, and goal attainment are directly impacted.

Planning personal time is now much easier with the aid of electronic handheld organizers that can store phone numbers, plan your schedule, and even prompt you when you have an appointment. For the technologically challenged, there is the more traditional "snail" method of using a pocket calendar. Whether paper or electronic, the first key to time management is to go out and buy a daily planner.

On Sunday evening think about the coming week. What activities will help you accomplish your goals? Make a list of these activities, and then schedule time in your planner to work on each. If you need to get a job, decide how you will structure your activities so that you can get a job quickly. Maybe there are family obligations that need to be met in the evening. If so, schedule time for them. Perhaps you and your spouse or friends are planning a night at the movies. Work activity and time at home to do chores are also parts of a seven-day schedule. Record days and times for all of these activities in a planner.

Remember, your goal is to fill your time, with positive, productive activities that you engage in on a regular, predictable basis. It is up to you to decide what changes in your schedule and routine need to be made so your week is predictable. Paying close attention to well-planned details will insure the outcome you desire. Always carry your planner with you as you would your wallet or handbag. Make adjustments and corrections in your schedule when you need to. At the close of each day, review your accomplishments. You now have created a structure to reinforce self-management and acquired yet another tool for self-control.

And Now ... Work

Human work is a complex process that has the potential to bring tremendous personal satisfaction. Mastering your addiction and maintaining recovery will facilitate work performance that will delight your supervisors, increase your self-esteem, and further reinforce your recovery. As Sigmund Freud said so long ago, "Work, more than any activity, has the potential for binding one closer to reality."

However, a high percentage of people who battle addictions are unemployed. In fact, the rate of unemployment is second only to people with mental illness. People with addictions who have had multiple attempts at alcohol/drug rehabilitation are more likely than not to have been fired from a job or asked to resign. Addiction disrupts your work life, resulting in lost productivity and lost wages.

When you are able to manage your addiction so it no longer interferes with your life, it's time to return to your job—that is, if you still have one.

If you have to change jobs or you are unemployed, then some of the potential obstacles you might encounter include anxiety about job interviews, finding the job that meets your expectations and your abilities, making the right impression on potential employees, and giving accurate answers to difficult job interview questions. Even so, pathways to finding a job and the resources to cope with those issues have never been easier or more accessible. Hundreds of excellent books on job searching, résumé, net working, interviewing, and other helpful topics are available to guide you through the process. Internet resources, too, are proliferating. We've recommended some of the best books and Web sites in the Resources section on pages 135–37.

Use the time management skills discussed earlier in the chapter to schedule time to devote to finding and maintaining satisfying work. We'll also discuss here some important points for recovering addicts to remember when searching for a job.

Personal Appearance

Your outward characteristics greatly influence how people respond to you. More importantly, your appearance suggests how you feel about yourself. It conveys a strong message to others—particularly people you meet for the first time—and first impressions are critically important during job interviews.

Do you dress for success? Are your fingernails clean, teeth brushed, hair combed, face shaved or beard trimmed? Is makeup applied tastefully? If you wear glasses, are the lenses clean? To get a good job you need to "sweat the small stuff." Attention to personal details and consistent hygiene are requisite self-care skills that enhance your appearance.

When networking or interviewing wear clothing that matches and is color coordinated. Clothing must be clean and free from wrinkles and food stains. A tie may be unnecessary, but a "collared" shirt for men is a must. Women should wear nonprovocative, conservative attire with lightly applied makeup to accentuate facial features. Most department stores gladly offer this service if you need help.

Consider the fact that even the color of clothing worn can tell others about you. Many marketing consultants advise top business executives to "dress for success" using the abbreviated guide below:

- Charcoal gray, black, or navy blue convey seriousness

- Bright colors like red or orange attract attention.

- Green conveys persistence.

- Yellow clothing should not be worn.

Clothing and style of dress adds to your marketing appeal and is especially important when returning to work or going on job interviews.

Attitude

In addition to appearance, part of your appeal has to be courtesy and manners. When meeting someone for the first time, make eye contact, shake hands firmly, and introduce yourself in an audible, upbeat tone, enunciating your words; don't mumble. Take initiative in your job or job search, and do for yourself what you need to do without being told. Remember, you are marketing yourself.

Having an energized attitude when you return to work will insure that you make a good adjustment and convey to others in a positive way your commitment to addiction-free health. The way you dress, your social graces, and the tone of your voice all increase ERP's effectiveness when returning to work or searching for a job.

INITIATIVE IN

MAINTAINING

ATTITUDE

GUARANTEES

EXCELLENCE

Just like the clothing you wear, your attitude is the "clothing for your personality." The image you project is an element of lifestyle that is completely self-regulated—completely under your control. It is up to you to take the initiative to project the appropriate image. Make the following phrase your mantra. "'Initiative' means taking responsibility voluntarily without being prompted."

How do you take this initiative? Begin by thinking about your attitudes about going back to work. What does your attitude convey? Are you curt, angry, hostile, and aggressive, or are you passive and slow to respond? What is your level of personal awareness? Are you in touch with your feelings?

Pay attention to yourself. Are you pleasant and conscientious in the workplace, or do you "cop an attitude"? Your attitude encourages positive or negative actions from those around you. For example, if you think people are always critical of you, then you are poised to react in a hostile manner—and to get hostility in return. If these kinds of negative attitudes are a problem for you, allow your negative attitudes to hibernate while you repeat a key phrase over and over in your head: *"I can do this . . . I will succeed in whatever I decide to do."* It's also reasonable to be humble, devoid of the bravado that characterized your addictive behavior. In a job interview, your objective is to convey willingness, dependability, and reliability to someone who doesn't know you. Your attitude needs to be consistent with these characteristics so that you convey how responsible an employee you will be.

Job Interviews

A common concern among recovering addicts is how to handle interview questions about their addictions. Make a list of what those questions might be and script out answers the night before. Keep your answers brief. Many addicted people feel they need to share intimate treatment details about their addictions. Don't! Treatment for your addiction is personal and carries too much social stigma to share with people you meet for the first time. Keep these details to yourself.

An interviewer may ask you about your *current* use of illegal drugs, because current use of illegal drugs is not protected under the Americans with Disabilities Act (ADA). Questions that relate to lawful drug use, such as, "Do you take methadone?" are excluded. An employer can ask about lawful drug use if she is administering a test for illegal drugs and the presence of legal drugs is discovered.

According to the ADA, "Persons who have completed or are currently participating in drug rehabilitation programs and who are no longer using illegal drugs are considered to be persons with disabilities." If you have been treated and are not currently using, then you can be considered disabled under ADA and may ask your employer for special accommodation (for example, to adjust work hours so you can attend AA). However, our experience has been that it is not in your best interests to do so. It is best to avoid discussing your treatment history with your prospective employer. Remember, questions about past drug or alcohol addiction are not permitted during the interview process. A job interviewer can ask if you have used illegal drugs, when you last used illegal drugs, and whether you have used illegal substances in the past six months. Questions about drinking habits are permitted, such as whether you drink or whether you have been arrested for a DUI or DWI. "How much do you drink?" is *not* allowed, as the answer may suggest alcoholism, a disability covered under ADA. This sounds a bit confusing. Just remember an employer *can* ask if you have used drugs or alcohol in the last six months. They *cannot* ask you if you are addicted to alcohol or drugs or if you have been treated for such an addiction.

The following table presents a more complete list of questions that an employer is prohibited from asking you under the rules of the ADA.

Questions an Employment Interviewer Is Prohibited from Asking

1. What is your marital status?

2. Do you have kids?

3. Do you have a disability? (You must disclose your disability at the time of the interview if you are seeking accommodation.)

4. What is your age?

5. Questions related to religious preference or sexual orientation

6. Questions related to ethnic background

7. Have you ever filed worker's compensation?

8. How much do you weigh and how tall are you?

9. Dates of high school or college attendance

10. How did you receive that scar?

11. Do you have any physical disabilities?

12. How many days were you out sick last year?

13. Do you or have you ever suffered from an emotional illness?

14. Have you ever been treated for alcohol or drug abuse?

15. Are you a veteran?

If any of these questions is asked, you may refuse to answer it, but be polite. Questions 3, 7, 10, 12, 13, and 14 may apply to people with substance abuse problems. Most corporate employers are aware of the fact that they cannot ask these questions. Small business owners may not be. Here is a sample dialog to help you frame an appropriate response to these questions.

Interviewer: Are you married?

You: Are you sure that you want me to answer that question? I read an article recently that said this is a question that may not be asked for a job interview. I think it has something to do with a federal law. Do you know if I am correct about this?

Interviewer: Have you ever filed for worker's compensation?

You: I am very interested in working for your company and I am in fine health. I understand from an article that I recently read that questions about disability are not allowed in interviews according to federal law. Am I wrong about this?

If you are asked any of these questions remain polite. Try to respond by first pointing out why you think you would be good at the job in question and then indicate very tentatively that you believe the law prohibits such questions. End by asking the interviewer if you are wrong about this. Help the interviewer to save face. Avoid accusing him of doing something wrong. If the interviewer persists in asking a forbidden question you have the option of answering it if it favors your cause or declining to do so if it does not.

Before an interview, you must also consider carefully what previous employers may have said about you if contacted. Did you do something that will result in negative information that can damage your chances for a new job? Could some difficult questions come up in the interview? If so, don't become manipulative as you were during your days of addiction. And don't lie or embellish. You will lose your job if it is discovered that you falsified information on your employment application or résumé. Companies check the veracity of the statements you make—don't kid yourself. Besides you have enough skeletons in your closet already. If you can answer the questions in the next table honestly and sincerely, you are ready for your first interview.

10 Difficult Questions That Require 10 Honest Answers

1. **Tell me about yourself.**
   Use real life experiences that illustrate how you have been persistent, ambitious, detailed oriented, motivated, energetic, and a quick learner. You should prepare a list of examples of each prior to interviewing.

2. **What caused you to change your jobs so many times?**
   Possible answers include: "I've been trying to find my niche"; "My former jobs didn't meet my expectations"; "Most of my recent work has been entry level, with no opportunity for advancement"; "I have the ability to be a very good worker who will be loyal to the company if given the opportunity."

3. **Have you ever been fired from a job and were you ever forced to quit to avoid being fired?**
   Here you have to make a choice. If you were fired due to the consequences of previous substance abuse and you are now in recovery, it is best to avoid answering this question by not including such jobs on your résumé or job application.

   If you need to reveal that you have been fired you can say that it was a humbling experience and that it happened when you were younger. You could add, if necessary, that it was warranted but that you learned from the experience and it hasn't happened since. However, do not lie about a job that you have listed on your résumé or job application.

4. **Why after X years of employment will your former employer only verify your time worked—why can't you get a reference?**
   "I believe that this is their policy because they are concerned about being sued if they say the wrong thing. They told us that this was their policy. I can provide a personal reference from so and so."

5. **Are you satisfied with your previous performance?**
   Obviously you want to answer this question in a strongly positive fashion. List why you believe that you were successful in your last job. Positive performance reviews, customer compliments, and supervisor compliments should be highlighted.

6. **What are your strengths/do you have the ability to perform this job?**
   Have at least five strengths listed in advance that you can rattle off. Strengths such as team player, hard worker who tries to get the details right, fast learner, accepts and welcomes feedback are good ones to talk about. Be sure that the strengths you discuss are ones that sincerely reflect your work performance.

7. **Describe your weaknesses.**
   The best weaknesses to discuss are those that imply strength, such as, "I am willing to work very long hours even though my spouse complains about it. I am a perfectionist about my work so sometimes it may take me a little longer to get things just right."

8. **How do you adapt your performance knowing what weaknesses you possess?**
   The best answers focus on seeking assistance from those who are good at what you are weak at.

9. **Why was your driver's license suspended?**

It is important to be truthful about this, but emphasize that you have made adjustments in your driving habits so this is no longer an issue. The best lead in to your answer is to ask if the job requires a driver's license. If the answer is no, reflect that fact in your response.

10. **What do you envision your life to be like in ten years?**

You want your answer to include that you have very positive expectations for your life. You are an optimist. That in the short run you expect to do very well in the job you are applying for and that if the right opportunities for growth present themselves you are looking to make a long-term commitment to an employer.

Volunteering

A final item of interest in the world of work is volunteer work. Volunteering can be a wonderful way to explore your interests and abilities. It can also be an easy way of making new friends. Volunteering can help you to feel good about yourself because you are giving your time freely to others. Finally, volunteering can help to fill holes in your schedule. Where can you volunteer? The choices are numerous: hospitals, nursing homes, hospices, day care centers, museums, and senior citizen centers. If you are politically inclined you can volunteer for work on a campaign or for your local political party. If causes are your thing, you can volunteer to improve the environment, save the whales, or reform campaign financing. A little research on your part will turn up limitless volunteer opportunities.

If you aren't ready to work, don't need to work, cannot work, or are looking to keep busy with something healthy and enjoyable—volunteering may work for you.

Credit Counseling Services

Many recovering people have allowed addiction to ruin their financial condition. Typically, their outstanding bills exceed their ability to pay. Their credit ratings are poor and they cannot get credit cards, loans, or mortgages. Essentially, they are on the verge of bankruptcy. An effective alternative to bankruptcy, which can go a long way toward repairing your credit rating, is credit counseling. A credit counseling organization contacts your creditors, gets them off your back, and sets up payment plans that you can afford. Their services are free. You can get information about free credit counseling by calling Credit Counseling Centers of America at 1-800-761-0061. Another free credit counseling service is AmeriDebt and they can be reached at 1-800-252-4800. They can help you if you have at least $2,000 in debt.

If your financial health is pretty good but you need more cost-effective forms of debt financing, a search on the Internet will help you find the best interest rate deals. At Web sites such as *www.bankrate.com* or *www.lendingtree.com*, you can research the best loan, mortgage, credit card, and other rates with just a click of your mouse. These sites make comparison shopping easy. Getting good information can help you to reduce your monthly expenses by consolidating debt and getting rid of high interest-rate credit cards.

Ex-Addiction Buddies

Your recovery will fail if you hang out with the people you partied with. No matter how much you want to continue your relationships with even one or two ex-buddies you must resist the temptation to do so. Relapse rates among people who try to quit run as high as seventy-five percent within one year. If you want to improve your odds you will avoid your addiction buddies. A second good reason for doing so is that your addiction buddies are not your real friends. Most recovering people will tell you that the people they partied with were upon reflection not their true friends. They needed someone to get high with, you wanted someone to get high with, and that was the core purpose of the relationship. It was one of mutual convenience—not of genuine friendship. Most people in recovery eventually realize that without the addiction there isn't anything left.

Chapter 5 provides you with important guidance on how you can get support for your recovery effort. Without a strong support network your chances of a successful recovery are very low. We want to repeat this. You cannot succeed in remaining clean and sober unless you have a very strong support group! Most recovering addicts tend to minimize their need for a support system. This is one reason most of them relapse.

Lifestyle Redesign Tips

We've gathered together some ideas suggested and used by people in recovery that helped them to re-engineer their lifestyles. Perhaps you'll find a suggestion or two that will help you too.

1. Have a fail-safe drink ready to order in party situations so you won't have to think about what to get.

2. Make a self-motivation tape you can play in your car to keep yourself strong. Be creative and make it interesting and fun.

3. Keep the phone numbers of your sponsor and two other recovery supporters in your wallet, in your car, and programmed into your cell phone (if you have one).

4. Join a gym to increase your healthy feelings.

5. Have lists of stress-reducing activities that you can use on a moment's notice: take a walk, take a jog, listen to tape of ocean waves, etc.

6. Join a chat group on the Internet for former substance abusers.

7. Take a continuing education class in a fun subject—something you've always wanted to learn to do.

8. Mail yourself motivating letters to keep your focus on recovery.

9. Start a hobby collecting something such as old toys, dolls, rocks, records, etc. Put the compulsiveness associated with substance abuse to work doing something healthy.

10. Get a natural high by trying to skydive, bungee jump, or ride river rapids.

11. Change your image: buy new clothes, change your hairstyle, change your facial hair, color your hair, etc.

12. When you feel cravings coming on, think of building a new house to live in. Focus all your mental energy on designing your own dream house. Sketch it out on some paper.

13. Set up a "Recovery Chart." Mark off each day you successfully stayed clean. After twenty-eight days treat yourself to something special (but healthy).

14. Have a complete physical at least every six months to ensure health.

15. Say hello to someone new every day.

16. Recite five positive affirmations or ERP cards daily.

17. Let yourself believe that you deserve positive changes in your life.

18. Set up scheduled and frequent pleasant social events (such as dinner out with a friend or other safe person) for keeping focused with recovery.

19. Take at least thirty minutes a day to meditate or relax in a quiet, stress-free area.

Come up with more ideas of your own. The more you think recovery, the stronger and more durable your recovery will be.

9

Protect Your Recovery

Reclaiming a lifestyle from the grasp of a self-destructive addiction requires a lifelong commitment. The opportunities for addictive indulgence will always be available as will your knowledge of how to access it. In some cases, your drug of choice will produce persistent changes in your brain chemistry that will take months to heal. Preserving and guarding your recovery is essential.

Millions of formerly addicted people have re-engineered a lifestyle free of addictive involvement. They have learned how to enjoy their lives without it. They have learned how to protect themselves from re-addiction. The focus of this chapter is how to prevent, minimize, and recover from relapses.

The first rule of relapse prevention is to expect to relapse.

The second rule of relapse prevention is to prove the first rule wrong.

The third rule of relapse prevention is to stop a *lapse* from becoming a relapse.

The final rule of relapse prevention is to celebrate the success of your recovery one day at a time.

Relapse Prevention Medications

There are no medications that will prevent a relapse. Medication cannot replace your determination to remain in recovery. There are, however, a couple of medications that may be of help to you. One such medication is called Revia (its generic name is naltrexone). The FDA has approved Revia for use by people who are trying to stay away from alcohol. Revia can help to reduce your cravings and thereby reduce future drinking. Revia cannot *stop* you from drinking, and this should be kept in mind if you decide to try it. If you are a narcotics user you cannot take Revia if you have used narcotics within the last three weeks—otherwise you will have a severe reaction. Revia is also used to help people addicted to opiates such as heroin. It works by totally blocking the euphoric effects of opiates. If you use opiates while taking Revia you will end up in the ER.

Antabuse (its generic name is disulfiram) has also been used to discourage people from consuming alcohol. If a person taking Antabuse drinks alcohol, he will get very sick. Unfortunately, any amount of alcohol—even in a mouthwash—could trigger a reaction. Additionally, Antabuse can cause drowsiness and liver complications in some people. Finally, Antabuse is only effective if you remember (or want) to take it daily. It is not a substitute for a genuine commitment to recovery.

Methadone and LAAM are used for people who cannot stay free of heroin use. Methadone must be taken daily, while LAAM can be taken several times per week. Neither can be abruptly discontinued without going through a withdrawal reaction. Methadone and LAAM substitute for heroin and block the brain receptor sites that heroin uses. A person on methadone must take it for the rest of her life or until she is ready to face life without it. It is an effective but partial treatment for heroin addiction.

There are no known medications that are of help to people who are addicted to cocaine, crack, or marijuana.

A medication in use in Europe and in clinical trials in the United States that may substitute for alcohol in a similar way that methadone substitutes for heroin is acamprostate (its brand name will be Campral). It may be approved for use in the United States around the year 2002.

For people who suffer from depression and anxiety unrelated to their substance abuse, there are a variety of antidepressant medications such as Paxil, Prozac, Effexor, and Celexa that can be of help. Anti-anxiety medications such as Buspar and Klonapin can help to reduce anxiety and agitation. People who are addiction prone, however, should be cautious about taking anti-anxiety medications such as Valium, Xanax, and Ativan, as they are potentially addictive. Klonapin can also be addictive. Buspar is nonaddictive but less effective.

If you believe that medication can be of assistance to you, consult your doctor.

Relapse Versus Re-Addiction

Relapse is not an all-or-nothing experience. There are many shades of gray in relapse. We identify three levels of relapse for our patients: lapse, relapse, and re-addiction. As we mentioned in an earlier chapter, the chances that you will experience some level of relapse are over seventy-five percent.

A lapse is a mess up. It is a one-time event where you give in to an impulse to use, realize that this is not what you want for yourself, and then take immediate action to prevent further substance abuse.

A relapse is defined as a lapse that extends for more than forty-eight hours. A relapse is prolonged. You may realize that you are in trouble, but it takes you awhile to take action to bring things back under control. You never give in fully to your relapse, however. A relapse is characterized by struggle against it.

A re-addiction is a relapse that gets completely out of your control—when you give in completely to substance abusing activities. You no longer want to stop. Any reluctance you may feel about what you are doing lasts only a few minutes at best. Most of your energy is focused on getting high and covering it up from the people who think that you are still in recovery.

Preventing re-addiction is the major goal of relapse prevention. It requires a three-pronged approach: relapse inoculation, relapse termination skills, and a re-addiction prevention pact.

Relapse Inoculation

The first, proactive step is to successfully complete a round of ERP therapy. Reducing your craving response to addiction cues is an essential part of being able to avoid a lapse in your recovery. Make sure you complete at least thirty ERP sessions (many addicts require up to sixty sessions). You should be able to view the set of ERP cards of your substance of choice without feeling a desire to use. When you have reached this goal you will know that you have done everything humanly possible to inoculate yourself from a lapse in recovery.

The second step is to effectively manage your daily schedule. During downtime, boredom and uncomfortable feelings can play tricks on your mind. Many formerly addicted people do not realize how much time they spent each day on acquiring, using, recovering from, and covering up their addictions. Once they are no longer involved in these activities they inherit a huge amount of time that needs to be filled. To manage your schedule, you need to get yourself an appointment calendar or day timer (see page 97).

It is very important that you schedule your day so that you are busy, especially during the times when you formerly got high. Plan your schedule at least three days in advance.

This way you will always have something to do at vulnerable times. Your schedule should include work, support group meetings, household chores, recreation activities, exercise, time with family and friends, and time for reflection and meditation. If you have more than two hours of unscheduled time during waking hours you should be concerned. Try to prevent this from happening. If you find that you are alone too often, adjust your schedule accordingly. Each morning review your schedule for the day. Make any changes required. Keep track of your schedule throughout the day. Check off scheduled items as you do them. Nightly, review your schedule for the next day. Every third night, plan your schedule for the following three days.

You should schedule yourself tightly for the first twelve months of recovery. After this your new lifestyle should be more comfortable and you can ease back a bit on scheduling all of your waking time.

The third step of proactive planning is to define the likely scenarios that could trigger you to use again. Most relapses are triggered by environmental events—such as boredom—that set off a struggle in your mind. You need to become aware of how you can mislead yourself into relapsing. One of the better ways of doing this is to write a *storyboard* that describes your next relapse. A storyboard is a series of drawings with captions that describes a sequence of actions. They are often used in the movie and television industry. To create one, draw as best as you can, using stick figures if necessary, a sequence of events that leads up to your relapse. In each panel of the storyboard, write an appropriate caption that describes what is happening. An eight-panel storyboard might look like the one on the following page:

Relapse Prevention Storyboard: Marijuana Use

Sitting home alone and feeling nervous and bored.	Started to think about getting high.	Called up Pete who always has pot.	Argued with myself about getting stoned.
Left my house to go to Pete's.	Pete hooked me up with a joint.	We smoked it and I got high.	When I came down, I felt lousy about relapsing.

Try your hand at describing how you might fall into a relapse. Don't worry about your drawing skills. Just use stick figures as we did. Try to think through how you would try to manipulate yourself into using again. Identify the triggers that you are most likely to encounter in your daily schedule. How would they start you down the path of a relapse?

Once you have designed your storyboard, think about how you could have intervened with yourself to abort the relapse. Remember your cognitive scripts. Where could you have done something different, perhaps something suggested in this book, to stop yourself from using your addictive activities? Circle the panel where you could make a change and write in an alternative caption. Then redesign your storyboard, now showing a different outcome: an aborted lapse. This exercise should be repeated a couple of times each with a different relapse storyboard. Doing this exercise will help you uncover the ways you might try to deceive yourself into relapsing. It also will help you to recognize triggering events quickly enough to do something about them. Here are two blank storyboards for you to photocopy and use.

My Relapse Prevention Storyboard

"The Lapse"

My Relapse Prevention Storyboard

"The Aborted Lapse"

Facing the Impulse and Winning

All relapses begin in your mind. You start relapsing in your mind long before you hunt down your substance of choice. Preventing a relapse means being alert to addicted thinking and taking steps to change your thoughts to ones that will help you maintain your sobriety. ERP therapy helps you to do this by associating your cognitive script with the impulse to use. The hope is that these new, more positive thoughts will be triggered when you are tempted to give in and use. Once they are triggered, you can use them to fight off the impulse to use and thereby control it.

Inevitably the day will come when you will be very tempted to give in to the impulse. When you are faced with this situation, you will have a few moments to decide how to handle it. Your mind will be racing with thoughts and feelings of using. The negative effects of addiction will be absent from your thoughts. This is when you are most vulnerable. To successfully control the impulse you must have a well-rehearsed strategy available. Following is a model strategy that you can use to win the "use or not use" debate.

Psychologically managing relapse impulses can be done in four related ways. First, dispute the expected benefits you receive from your addictive activity. Second, distract your thinking with something totally unrelated to the urges. Third, change your physical environment. Fourth, reframe your ability to tolerate the urges.

As soon as you feel an urge to use your addictive activity, turn on your self-protection machine and challenge the urge. Here is where you will want to remember your ERP cognitive scripts. If you completed a sufficient number of sessions, the scripts should pop into your mind. Repeat them to yourself. Then say, out loud if necessary, "I do not want to use! I can control the impulse!"

In addition to thinking about your cognitive scripts ask yourself these questions:

- How will I feel later if I give in now?

- What are the negative consequences of giving in to the impulse?

- How am I trying to convince myself to get high? What rationalizations am I using?

- What bad things happened to me in the past because of this addictive activity?

- Don't I know that I can ride the Craving Wave and that it will go away?

Once you have successfully started to dispute the impulse, try to distract your thinking with something irrelevant. For example, count down from 100 by threes. Plan a really exciting vacation somewhere. Go out and take a brisk walk. Write a poem. Call a friend, support group member, or therapist for help. Think about your favorite movie star or hero. Imagine that you have been elected president of the United States, what laws would you like to see passed? Create your own "Distractions List" that you can carry with you and pull out in time of need. It is easy to do and a lot of fun. Be creative and enjoy yourself.

Your third strategy is to change your physical environment. Cravings are conditioned to physical stimuli. By changing your environment you change your thoughts and feelings. The change could be as simple as taking a warm shower or going for a brisk walk. It could be inviting a safe friend over for coffee or going shopping at the mall. It may even be going to a church or temple to pray or meditate. The type of change you will need to break the impulse very much depends on your history of chemical use. An environment that has never been associated with chemical use is the one you want. You should make a list today of your safe environments so you'll have them ready when you need them. Keep the list in your wallet.

The final step is to reframe your ability to tolerate your impulses. ERP has helped you to do this by showing you that your cravings can be extinguished. Instead of saying things like, "I can't stand it. They are too strong for me. This feels unbearable! I just have to give in," you can place the impulses in a completely different framework. Impulses to use mean that you are in recovery. They are proof positive of your commitment to taking strong action on your own behalf to enjoy a better life. They reflect how strong a person you really are. They are not temptations. They are signs of courage and inner strength. *If you can experience the craving impulse (without using) that means you are getting better!* Convince yourself of this in your own words. In so doing you will greatly increase you ability to tolerate your impulse.

Once you have successfully resisted an impulse, praise yourself for a job well done. Take your recovery one temptation and one day at a time and you will enjoy a much better quality of life.

Finally, if you slip and get high, don't let a single lapse turn into a relapse. Don't take a fuck-it-all attitude and go on a binge. Worse yet, don't let a lapse talk you into the idea that it is okay to use every now and then if your recovery goal is total abstinence. The best way to prevent a lapse from becoming a relapse is to tell someone in your support network what happened. This will allow you to talk things out and get needed support.

The Re-Addiction Pact

The final approach to relapse prevention is to devise a "re-addiction pact" with yourself that you will implement if you cannot put a relapse to an end. A re-addiction pact is your last line of defense against becoming re-addicted. It involves giving another person whom you trust the power to help you abort a relapse. You can structure your pact in a variety of ways. You can make a "watch only in the case of emergency videotape" in which you start out by saying, "If you are watching this tape, you are in the middle of a nasty relapse. . . ." The tape should motivate you to abort the relapse. You could instruct your trusted friend as follows: "Check in with me at least weekly, and if you think that I am relapsing make me watch the tape." If you refuse to watch the tape, then your pact with them could authorize them (in writing) to tip off the police about your illegal activities (this will get your attention). An alternative to police notification might be to have them notify family members, sponsor, and therapist that you are relapsing and to plan a family intervention in which you will be lovingly confronted about your behavior. After the confrontation, if you haven't aborted the relapse by getting additional treatment help, then your family and trusted friend will refuse to enable you and will cut off all forms of financial and housing assistance until you agree to treatment.

If some of these suggestions sound extreme, it is because they need to be so. They are your last-ditch attempt to abort re-addiction. By setting up a strong re-addiction pact you are helping yourself stay in recovery. So you need to think about what will really work for you. If you cannot bring yourself to set up a powerful re-addiction pact then chances are better than even money that, deep in your mind, you want to leave the door to re-addiction open—if only just a crack (no pun intended).

Strengthen Your Recovery by Reclaiming the Truth

The first casualty of addiction is the truth. The second casualty is the numbing of your emotions and feelings. Early in your recovery you will face an emotional wall composed of numbing seduction. The wall is there to stop your recovery from continuing. It was built by your addicted self—the same self that this very moment wants you to return to the "good" times before your addiction got out of control, when you enjoyed your high. All addicts long to return to those days, the days before they were addicted. Being in recovery doesn't shut down that desire in the least.

Some addicts are so eager to "recover" that they sweep all their painful feelings under the rug. They act as if everything is fine! Their addiction has been conquered—they will never relapse again. You can trust them again. They'll never hurt you again. They'll rebuild their life—it won't be hard. They are not worried. Everything will work out fine. The problem is that they are in denial about how difficult a true recovery really is. They are setting themselves, and anyone who believes them, up for a huge letdown. They will relapse, and they will do so sooner rather than later.

Only the truth will set you free to truly recover. But the truth hurts; a fantasy attitude about recovery is a lot easier to live with. Only the truth, however, will allow you to heal all of the psychological pain you have caused yourself and those you love.

The emotional wall that you face feels hopeless and depressing (that is how you will know that you are close to it). You have to feel those painful emotions. You have to feel the hurt and loss. Saying you do isn't enough. You must feel the pain. You must cry, feel incredibly sad, and seek out the forgiveness of those you have hurt. You must make amends with those you love or you will relapse. You must feel your pain, get humble, and seek forgiveness. If you don't, the pain inside will get you high again. And that is the unavoidable truth!

Find Meaning in Your Life

One of the recovery principles of Alcoholics Anonymous (AA) is the recognition of the need to turn control of your life over to your higher power. This principle is based on the idea that recovery requires an admission that your life is out of control and that you must therefore surrender all control of your life to God or your higher power. The act of surrendering control allows many people to feel a burden lifted from their shoulders. It allows them to draw a psychological line between their addicted life of the past and their recovering life of the present. In addition, reflection on a higher power leads naturally to a consideration of the meaning of one's life. What greater purpose does your life serve? What is important to you now that you are recovering? How much value do you place on being alive? Why were you placed on this planet? At this point in your recovery these are important questions to consider regardless of whether you consider yourself to be a religious person. You may want to start a diary to record your reflections about the meaning of your life and what role your recovery plays in your life going forward.

Your belief in God may be structured by one of the organized religions, it may find a very personal form of expression, or it may be entirely absent. Regardless of the state of your spiritual beliefs, we believe that some form of meditative reflection on the awesome power and scale of the Universe and the wonder of the gift of life is helpful to a successful recovery. So we offer you a meditative, religion-free prayer that you can use to stimulate your own inner reflection.

A Meditation Moment

Start with ten slow deep breaths, then close your eyes and repeat to yourself:
Everything is good. Everything is great.
Do it right. Do it without guilt.
Love and respect others. Protect and love yourself.
Seek to understand the You in Universe.
Respect and honor the Universe.
Amen.

We recommend that you repeat this meditation several times each day. Reflect on its meaning for you and your life. Write down in your diary any thoughts or feeling this form of reflective meditation sparks. Perhaps this process will help you to find your spiritual center. And if it does, your life could be transformed in a miraculous way.

Celebrate Your Recovery Milestones

The most important tactic for relapse prevention is to celebrate each recovery milestone. The first milestone is one week clean. The second is thirty days clean. The third milestone is ninety days clean. Then comes the six-month and one-year anniversaries. Your five-year anniversary is a very important one. Research has shown that people who have remained in recovery for five years are very unlikely to relapse.

Of course, you cannot get to these milestones by thinking about them too far in advance. One of the great pieces of AA wisdom is that recovery can only be achieved by focusing on it one day at a time. Putting lots of pressure on yourself to make your one-year anniversary will not help you to reach it. Focusing on today and handling it the right way will help you to achieve each of these milestones all in due time.

As you reach your milestones, share your accomplishments with others and plan a celebration. Go out to dinner, buy yourself something nice, or take a day off from work. Enjoying your recovery in healthy ways will reinforce your efforts and will make succeeding tomorrow just a little bit easier.

10

Enjoying What You Really Want

A successful recovery enables people to discover more about themselves than they ever thought possible. They learn about why they got addicted. They learn about what they really want from their lives. They learn who their true friends are. They learn about love—the love of others and the love of self. Recovery isn't about giving up an addictive pleasure; it's about discovering what really matters.

Over the years we have worked with hundreds of people who sought to overcome an addiction. We'd like to share with you the stories of a few of these people. Not all of these stories have a happy ending. But even unsuccessful attempts at recovery contain important lessons that others can benefit from.

Sarah—Ten Years Clean and Counting

Sarah is a thirty-seven-year-old woman who is in her tenth year of recovery from dependence on alcohol and pills. She went through several attempts at recovery before she was able to achieve her current success. She lost a marriage along the way. Her ex-husband also drank, but he was a social drinker. During the period of her divorce her resolve to stay clean started to slip. She promptly sought help and was able to emotionally navigate through this difficult time without drinking or taking drugs. In the process she started to deal with her history of psychotraumatic events, which she had avoided for years. This involved family therapy sessions with mother and sisters. Her father was an alcoholic and was often very abusive to family members. With these issues behind her, Sarah was able to get on with her life. She got a new job in the computer services field and a new boyfriend. She feels good about what she has accomplished and is very optimistic about the future. Her treatment plan included AA, ERP therapy, individual psychotherapy, group therapy, family therapy, and lots of reading.

John—From Addict to Chef

John started treatment at age fifteen. He had been hospitalized several times for depression, suicide attempts, and polysubstance abuse. His childhood was very psychotraumatic. His father was extremely physically and psychologically abusive toward John, his mother, and his siblings. Eventually, he abandoned the family. John used alcohol, cocaine, and marijuana to cope with these stressful feelings and traumatic memories. At age nineteen he received residential treatment for about nine months followed by several months of outpatient care. This enabled him to sort out his feelings, reduce his need to abuse drugs and alcohol, and figure out what he wanted to do with his life. ERP helped him to reduce his impulse to use, and group and individual psychotherapy helped him with his emotions. The residential program provided him with a supportive environment that he never had at home. John decided to attend the Culinary Institute of America to learn to become a chef. He graduated in three years and started what has become a very successful career doing something he enjoys.

Mary—A Trauma-Driven Addiction

Mary is a thirty-five-year-old woman who had a history of six previous hospitalizations over the past seven years. Her chief reason for being admitted was the fact that she was feeling depressed, and suicidal, and she was drowning her feelings with alcohol. Mary reported drinking daily for the last year or so, but the amount slowly progressed up from a few beers a day to at least a twelve-pack a day. She had never really been addicted to other drugs, but had on occasion smoked marijuana.

Mary was raised in a middle-class family from the South. According to Mary, she had a happy childhood until she was eight. At that time a family member sexually abused her. This trauma caused Mary to feel guilty and ashamed, and her self-confidence and self-esteem dropped dramatically. She began to experiment with drugs and alcohol at the age of twelve or thirteen. She found that drinking eased her "bad" feelings. This continued to progress and when Mary was twenty-two her addiction affected every aspect of her life. Mary lost several key jobs due to her drinking, had a hard time establishing a positive relationship with her family, and most difficult of all, lost her son due to her drinking. Mary allowed her mother to care for her teenage son because her drinking was now beginning to affect their relationship. He had no respect for her, was very angry with her, and would not listen to her.

When Mary was introduced to ERP, she was open minded to anything that might help her. She responded favorably to the ERP therapy sessions. However, Mary was surprised by her initial physical reactions to the ERP sessions. These reactions included watery mouth, sweaty palms, and a high pulse rate. Mary was able to memorize the cognitive scripts with ease. She participated in AA meetings, individual and group therapy, and most importantly, was placed in a personality disorder group to work on the abuse issues from her past. According to Mary this all-around treatment package worked well in helping her to understand herself better and to control her addiction.

Mary has been clean and sober for one and a half years since being discharged from the residential program. She has re-established a healthy and positive relationship with her family as well as with her son. He currently lives with her and both are able to express their feelings to each other. This was accomplished after several months of family therapy and individual counseling. Mary remains gainfully employed and recently received a promotion for her excellent work. She reported that her attendance at AA meetings could be better, but she has replaced those missed meetings with college classes and other extracurricular activities that she finds interesting (writing classes, pottery classes, and dance classes).

Ron—Cleaning Out the Madness

Ron is an eighteen-year-old man who was hospitalized three times in the previous two years for his drug problem. Ron admitted to smoking marijuana daily for the six to seven months prior to his treatment at SLS Health. At his peak, he was smoking two to three joints per day. In the past Ron experimented with other drugs (cocaine, alcohol, and LSD) but always returned to marijuana. Marijuana smoking eventually made him paranoid, and this triggered his hospitalizations.

Ron was raised in an upper-middle-class family and was the youngest of four boys. His family was supportive and loving to him all his life. Ron got hooked up with a few friends who introduced him to marijuana when he was thirteen or fourteen. Ron continued to use marijuana frequently while he was at a private school. Prior to his senior year, Ron was diagnosed with schizoaffective disorder during one of his hospitalizations. Ron admitted to hearing voices and having some racing thoughts, symptoms he discovered were reduced when he smoked marijuana. It was after this admission that he was introduced to ERP.

When Ron first began ERP, he was skeptical, unsure, and leery about how it was going to work for him. After his first session, Ron began to respond by eagerly memorizing his cognitive scripts. More importantly he began to establish control over his cravings, and he found new ways to deal with his feeling of inadequacy. In conjunction with individual psychotherapy, medication management, drug and alcohol education, as well as with the support of his family, Ron started to get the picture. He made a conscious choice to stay clean and sober.

Ron was discharged from treatment after six months. He returned to high school where he graduated as scheduled—drug and alcohol free. After graduation, Ron returned to live with his parents for six to seven months in order to save up money to go to college. Ron is currently at a culinary school in upstate New York where he is pursing his dream of becoming a chef. He continues to see an outpatient therapist and psychiatrist who have been working on reducing his symptoms. Ron left treatment at SLS two and a half years ago, and he remains clean to this day. Ron can still recite thirteen of the eighteen original cognitive scripts.

Scott—Driven to Party

Scott did not have a strong personal commitment to recovery. His mother pushed him into treatment and he went along with it. He was about twenty at the time. Scott was adopted at age four. Neglect, abuse, and several foster placements characterized his years from birth to adoption. His adoptive family was very loving, but by the time they got Scott he was very hyperactive and emotionally distant. They saw to it that Scott received a good education and had a very comfortable home. Unfortunately, Scott got himself involved with "bad" kids and picked up his drug and alcohol habit. He was a handsome and charming young man and he used this to get what he wanted from others. He enjoyed partying—the drugs, sex, and good times. His parents tried to get him help on a number of occasions. He complied with treatment when he had to, but he got little out of it. By the time he came to us, he was facing drug possession charges. He cooperated with the program at a superficial level, but he never made a commitment to change. He still enjoyed his addiction and saw no reason of his own for changing his behavior. He went along with ERP, individual and group therapy, and so forth. When he was discharged he moved to Florida and continued to party. He has been hospitalized several times since then.

Sam—Persistence Despite Relapse

Sam is a twenty-five-year-old male who was admitted to our facility after being hospitalized ten times in the past three years. He was hospitalized for depression and drug addiction. Sam began to use crack seven months prior to his last hospitalization. Sam had been using crack daily for the past two of those seven months, using three to four times per day. Sam spent all his time, energy, and money on planning and getting the "ultimate high."

Sam had been raised in a middle-class family on Long Island. His parents were divorced when he was five years old, and it was a bitter divorce. Sam knew there were problems with his upbringing even at an early age. He felt the tension, remembered the arguments, and even blamed himself years later. This type of upbringing led Sam to have difficulties at school (truancy, conduct problems, and drugs). He also got in trouble with the law at the age of fourteen. Sam started with alcohol, progressed to marijuana and eventually began to experiment with heroin, cocaine, crack, LSD, and PCP. This progression continued until his high school graduation, when he admitted himself into a detox for the first time.

When Sam was introduced to ERP, it was extremely difficult for him to accept the idea of never using drugs or alcohol again. Sam did not believe he would be able to control himself in the ERP room and was skeptical about the whole process. After the initial sessions, Sam began to see that there was a chance for recovery. This was the first time Sam had ever held a crack pipe and not used it. His self-control and self-esteem increased with each session. Sam was able to handle the paraphernalia and memorize the cognitive scripts—all in about two weeks. This confidence boost led Sam to attend Narcotics Anonymous meeting and to seriously begin to work on his recovery. Sam realized, with the assistance of ERP and individual and group therapy, several important factors about himself. First, he realized that he was really a good person inside but had made bad choices. Next, he understood how all of the angry feelings he aimed at his family contributed to his addiction. Lastly, he could see that his negative self-image was slowly changing for the better.

Sam was discharged from our residential program and transferred to our structured outpatient program. During the structured outpatient phase Sam was accepted to college and found employment. Sam continued to attend Narcotics Anonymous and met with his therapist on a regular basis. However, there was a time during that phase that he relapsed. Sam admitted to smoking marijuana on numerous occasions. Sam reported that there was a period when his stress level was overwhelming and he reverted to his old behaviors. Sam reported that there were no occasions of using cocaine or crack.

Sam truthfully admitted his relapse and was able to get back on track with his treatment. Since then, Sam has moved into his own apartment, bought a car on his own, continued to support himself financially, and quickly moved up to a management position at work. Since his relapse he has remained clean and sober and feels very good about it.

The Six Ingredients for Success

Our years of experience with helping people of all ages and walks of life to achieve an addiction-free life has taught us that a successful recovery has six characteristics. We would like to share them with you. We hope that this information will help you to better manage your recovery effort.

The first ingredient is a strong, focused, and optimistic personal conviction that the time has come to change. This conviction develops once you realize that the costs of your addiction far outweigh their advantages and pleasures. There is no room for ambivalence! Until a person comes to this conclusion without outside coercion—however well meaning it is—they will continue to use despite receiving the best treatment available. Personal commitment also requires an optimistic outlook about your prospects for overcoming addiction. If your subconscious does not expect success, then success will be very hard to achieve. You need to be totally honest with yourself and with everyone who is part of your support network. If you are, then you will cultivate the optimistic commitment you need to change.

The second ingredient is having the support of others. We spoke about this earlier in this book. Research has shown that this is one of the most important factors for achieving a successful recovery. The reason is fairly obvious: you need to know that someone cares enough about you to want you to kick your habit. Serious addiction lowers your self-esteem. To get clean and stay clean, you need to care about yourself. If your addicted state of mind limits your ability to care about yourself, then the love and care of another can help a great deal. It can get you started on the road to recovery and self-esteem. However, virtually no one gets sober because another person wants her to. The decision to live a sober life can only be made because *you* want it that way. You'll never get sober for someone else, but people who care about you can help your recovery once you've decided to commit yourself to it. Remember, too, that support groups such as AA and NA can also be integral parts of a successful recovery plan.

The third ingredient is overcoming the impulse to use. The longer your addiction has existed the more associations you have formed between everyday stimulus situations and the impulse to use—and the more your recovery will depend on breaking these connections. ERP therapy will help you to do this. The more sessions you complete, the weaker the impulse to use will become. It is that simple. The use of medications such as Revia or Antabuse can also be very helpful.

The fourth ingredient is dealing effectively with your psychological issues. If you have any of the following, they must be treated: guilt about those you hurt, depression, anxiety, mood swings, psychosis, personality disorder, or a history of past psychotrauma. *If you hate who and what you are, you will never stay clean no matter how many times you try.* Without treatment you will be very vulnerable to relapse, because addiction is a refuge from the negative feelings stirred up by self-hatred and related problems. If you have a history of psychological trauma, have been diagnosed with a personality disorder, or grew up in a very dysfunctional family, then you may be interested in reading *The Angry Heart*, by Dr. Joe Santoro and Dr. Ronald Cohen (1997). The book deals with the issues of trauma and dysfunctional childhoods and how they often lead to substance abuse problems. It provides you with a step-by-step way to overcome the emotional effects of these problems.

Help with your psychological problems is a phone call or e-mail away. If you have never consulted a therapist, do not be afraid (or ashamed) to do so. A therapist is someone who will hold everything you say absolutely confidential and who can give you honest feedback (because they do not want or need anything from you except their fee). A good therapist is worth his weight in gold. He can really help you develop a healthier and happier lifestyle. To find a therapist near you, go to *www.slshealth.com*'s therapist search engine. It is free of charge.

The fifth ingredient is discovering what you truly enjoy in life. It could be as simple as a quiet sunrise or as involved as getting a Ph.D. It is important that you fill your days with healthy activities that you enjoy doing. There will always be the routine things, the chores, and the responsibilities that must be done. What we are talking about is finding those things that put a smile on your face. A secret passion, a hobby, a quiet pastime that you have long ignored or never knew was in you. Visit our Web site at *www.killthecraving.com*. There you will find over one hundred ideas in the form of magazines that are devoted to one special interest that can help you find a new passion. Perhaps you will discover something there that will more than fill the void created by the end of your addiction.

The final ingredient for success is luck. Luck plays a factor in all human enterprises, great and small alike. The same is true for a recovery effort. Good luck is an essential success factor, but it is completely outside of your control. A patient of ours was well advanced in his recovery until his mother told him that she was a lesbian and that she was going to move in with her female lover. This came as quite a shock to him and caused a relapse that took him several more years to recover from. Events such as this are truly beyond your control—but knowing this is not enough to stop them from interfering with your recovery. The best protection against this type of relapse is to work with a psychotherapist. These types of events need to be discussed in a frank and confidential fashion. When you are inside a therapy session, the emotions that are stirred up by unlucky events can be neutralized so they will be less likely to trigger a relapse.

Of course, luck could also run in your favor and support your recovery. Meeting a very special person or getting an excellent job is an example of good luck that can make a significant difference. Let's hope for more good luck than bad.

A Daily Beginning . . .

If you can combine these six ingredients for success together with the right timing, you will be among those who successfully recover from serious drug and alcohol addiction. If you do not succeed the first time, try to remember that on average it takes seven attempts before someone is able to remain clean and sober. The lesson is clear: Be persistent and learn from your mistakes, and you will achieve a better and more satisfying way of life. Take your recovery one day at a time and, most importantly, enjoy your recovery and your new lifestyle. We hope that your higher power and good fortune guide your way.

Let us know how you're doing. We'd love to hear from you. You can contact us at 1-888-8-CARE-4U or on the Web at *www.killthecraving.com*.

A

Here and Now Craving Scales

Alcohol Cravings Version

Level	Description of Craving
10	Even if you tried to stop me, I would do anything (steal, prostitute myself, harm others) to drink.
9	Even if you tried to stop me, I would try to leave now and drink.
8	I want to leave now and drink. I'm really craving hard.
7	If I were in the community, I would try to drink.
6	If someone offered me alcohol, I would drink it.
5	If someone offered me my favorite type of alcohol, I would drink it.
4	If someone offered me alcohol, I might drink.
3	If someone offered me alcohol, I might not drink.
2	If someone offered me alcohol, I would not drink.
1	If someone offered me alcohol, I would definitely refuse it and not drink.
0	I no longer have any desire to drink. Alcohol is poison. I will never drink again.

Drug Cravings Version

Level	Description of Craving
10	Even if you tried to stop me, I would do anything (steal, prostitute myself, harm others) to get high.
9	Even if you tried to stop me, I would try to leave now and get high
8	I want to leave now and get high. I'm really craving hard.
7	If I were in the community, I would try to get high.
6	If someone offered me drugs, I would get high.
5	If someone offered me my favorite type of drug, I would get high.
4	If someone offered me drugs, I might get high.
3	If someone offered me drugs, I might not get high.
2	If someone offered me drugs, I would not get high.
1	If someone offered me drugs, I would definitely refuse it and not get high.
0	I no longer have any desire to get high. Drugs are poison. I will never get high again.

Resources

Internet Information and Support

http://www.killthecraving.com As a reader of this book you can access the *www.killthecraving.com* site to do photo card ERP, get E-mail Counselor advice, or chat online. Information about treatment programs and educational information about substance abuse is also available at the site. Your password is the last five digits of this book's ISBN number, and your user name is "bookreader." Once on the site you can create a unique user name and password for yourself.

http://www.slshealth.com This site provides information and online counseling services as well as a free two-question professional advice service called the E-mail Therapist.

http://www.hubplace.com/addictions/ This site describes itself in the following manner: "Addiction Resource Guide is a new Internet company whose mission is to help professionals and consumers find resources for dealing with addictive problems. We are excited about the possibilities as we build our company and provide a service that we know would not otherwise be available." The site lists treatment facilities by geographic location and subspecialty.

http://www.r-a.org/— This site describes itself as a "Twelve-Step Fellowship designed especially for those who have searched for recovery in other programs, but have thus far not found it as well as for those who may have found some recovery but are frustrated by the endless discussion of, and upon, self-destructive behavior and personal problems." They take a more practical and less perfectionist view of the recovery process. Their approach is spiritually oriented.

http://www.arf.org/— This site is from Canada and provides information, a safe drinking questionnaire, and drug-use statistics in an easy-to-navigate format.

http://www.mlode.com/~ra/— This site offers topics related to recovery issues, such as abusive upbringings, anger, family violence, and finding a balance in life. Articles are thought provoking.

The Web is an expanding network of resources that one day will link all of us to each other. Ten years ago this resource was available only to a few computer nerds. Today anyone can benefit from it. We hope that you will make it part of your support network.

Support Groups

Alcoholics Anonymous, World Service, Inc.
General Service Office
P.O. Box 459
Grand Central Station
New York, NY 10163
(212) 870-3400

Benzodiazepine Anonymous
BA
11633 San Vicente Blvd., Suite 314
Los Angeles, CA 90049
(310) 652-4100

Cocaine Anonymous
CA
3740 Overland Ave., Suite C
Los Angeles, CA 90034-6334
(800) 347-8998

Marijuana Anonymous
MA
P.O. Box 2912
Van Nuys, CA 91404
(800) 766-6779

Men for Sobriety and Women for Sobriety
P.O. Box 618
Quakertown, PA 18951-0618
(215) 536-8026

Moderation Management
Moderation Management
P.O. Box 27558
Golden Valley, MN 55427
(612) 512-1484

Narcotics Anonymous
NA
P.O. Box 9999
Van Nuys, CA 91404
(818) 773-9999

Pill Addicts Anonymous
Pill Addicts Anonymous
P.O. Box 13738
Reading, PA 19612-3738

Rational Recovery
Rational Recovery Systems
P.O. Box 800
Lotus, CA 95651
(916) 621-4374
(800) 303-2873

SLS Health
This site offers mental health information and self-guided treatment advice. It also features the E-mail Therapist, which provides professional advice by e-mail.
2503 Carmel Ave
Dept 279
Brewster, NY 10509
1-888-8-CARE-4U
www.slshealth.com

SMART (Self Management and Recovery Training)
SMART
24000 Mercantile Rd., Suite 11
Beachwood, Ohio 44122
(216) 292-0220

Employment-Related Web Sites

- Monster.com

- HotJobs.com

- AOL workplace: AOL key word *jobs*

- Careermosaic.com—Recently combined with headhunter.net, offering access to over 10,000 companies. This comprehensive site helps you manage your résumé and track its effectiveness.

- CareerPath.com—Has employment listing from newspapers from around the country.

There are many more employment-related Web sites and you can explore the Internet for hours in your quest for the perfect job.

Reclaiming Your Lifestyle

We've included a list of books that can help you redesign your lifestyle along the lines discussed in chapter 8. Check them out online at *www.amazon.com* for reviews and reader ratings.

F., Dan. 1991. *Sober but Stuck: Obstacles Most Often Encountered That Keep Us from Growing in Recovery.* Minneapolis: Compcare Publishers.

Goines, D. 1991. *Dopefiend.* Los Angles: Holloway House.

Helfand, D. 1995. *Career Change Everything You Need to Know to Meet New Challenges and Take Control of Your Career.* Chicago: VGM Career Horizons.

Kuhn, C., S. Swaltzweldwe, and W. Wilson. 1998. *Buzzed: The Straight Facts About the Most Used and Abused Drugs from Alcohol to Ecstasy.* New York: W. W. North & Company.

Richmond, C. A. 1997. *Twisted: Inside the Mind of a Drug Addict.* New Jersey: Jason Aronson Inc.

Waldorff, D., C. G. Reinarman, and S. Murphy. 1991. *Cocaine Changes. The Experience of Using and Quitting.* Philadelphia: Temple University Press.

Yablonsky, L. 1997. *The Story of Junk.* Boston: Little, Brown, & Company.

Twerski, A. J., and C. G. Nakken. 1997. *Addictive Thinking and the Addictive Personality.* New York: MJF Books.

Singer, J. A. 1969. *Message in a Bottle: Stories of Men and Addiction.* New York: The Free Press.

Career Planning and Assessment

Bolles, R. N. 2000. *How to Find Your Mission in Life*. Berkeley, Calif.: Ten Speed Press.

————. 2000. *What Color is Your Parachute? 2000*. Berkeley, Calif.: Ten Speed Press.

Boulter, N., M. Daziel, and J. Hill. 1998. *Achieving the Perfect Fit: How to Win with the Right People in the Right Jobs*. Houston: Gulf Publishing Company.

Charland, W., and D. E. Henderson. 1998. *The Complete Idiot's Guide to Changing Careers*. New York: MacMillan Distribution.

Field, S. 2000. *100 Best Careers for the 21st Century*, 2nd ed. Arco Publications.

Kleiman, C. 1994. *The 100 Best Jobs for the '90s and Beyond*. New York: Berkeley Publishing Group.

Kranninch, R. 1999. *Change Your Job, Change Your Life: High Impact Strategies for Finding Great Jobs in the Decade Ahead*, 7th ed. Manassas Park, Va.: Impact Publications.

O'Connor, L. 1998. *Top Ten Dumb Career Mistakes*. Chicago: VGM Career Horizons.

Tieger, P. T., and B. Barron-Tieger. 1995. *Do What You Are: Discover the Perfect Career for You Through the Secrets of Personality Type*. New York: Little, Brown, & Company.

Interviewing

Fry, R. 2000. *101 Great Answers to the Toughest Interview Questions*. Franklin Lakes, N.J.: Career Press.

Hawk, B. S. 1998. *What Employers Really Want: The Insider's Guide to Getting a Job*. Chicago: VGM Career Horizons.

Mornell, P., et al. 2000. *Games Companies Play: The Job Hunter's Guide to Playing Smart and Winning Big in the High Stakes Hiring Game*. Berkeley, Calif.: Ten Speed Press.

Tullier, M. 1999. *The Unofficial Guide to Acing the Interview*. IDG Books Worldwide.

Verucki, P. 1996. *The Adams Job Interview Almanac*. Holbrook, Mass.: Adams Media Corporation.

————. 1999. *The 250 Job Interview Questions You'll Most Likely Be Asked*. Holbrook, Mass.: Adams Media Corporation.

Resume and Cover Letters

Beatty, R. 1996. *The Perfect Cover Letter*, 2nd ed. New York: John Wiley and Sons.

Diggs, A. D. 1999. *Barrier Breaking Résumés and Interviews*. New York: Times Books.

Farr, J. M. 1995. *The Quick Resume and Cover Letter Book: Write and Use an Effective Resume in One Day*. Indianapolis: JIST Works.

Parker, Y. 1999. *The Damn Good Resume Guide: A Crash Course in Resume Writing*. Berkeley, Calif.: Ten Speed Press.

References

Baker, T. B., E. Morse, and J. E. Sherman. 1987. The motivation to use drugs: A psychobiological analysis of urges. In C. Rivers, ed. *Nebraska Symposium on Motivation* 34, 257–323.

Brown, S. B., and R. Hester. 1999. *The Assessment and Treatment of Psychoactive Substance Use Disorders*. La Jolla: University of San Diego.

Drummond, D. C., S. T. Tiffany, and B. Remington. 1995. *Addictive Behaviour: Cue Exposure Theory and Practice*. London: John Wiley and Sons, Ltd.

Santoro, J., and R. J. Cohen. 1997. *The Angry Heart: Overcoming Borderline and Addictive Disorders*. Oakland: New Harbinger Publications.

Santoro, J., R. DeLetis, and M. McNamara. *The Effects of Cue-Reactivity (Exposure Response Prevention) on Controlling Addictive Cravings*. Unpublished manuscript.

Tiffany, S. T. 1990. A cognitive model of drug urges and drug-use behavior: The role of automatic and non-automatic processes. *Psychological Review* 97, 147–168.

Some Other New Harbinger Self-Help Titles

Juicy Tomatoes, $13.95
Help for Hairpullers, $13.95
The Anxiety & Phobia Workbook, Third Edition, $19.95
Thinking Pregnant, $13.95
Rosacea, $13.95
Shy Bladder Syndrome, $13.95
The Adoption Reunion Survival Guide, $13.95
The Queer Parent's Primer, $14.95
Children of the Self-Absorbed, $14.95
Beyond Anxiety & Phobia, $19.95
The Money Mystique, $13.95
Toxic Coworkers, $13.95
The Conscious Bride, $12.95
The Family Recovery Guide, $15.95
The Assertiveness Workbook, $14.95
Write Your Own Prescription for Stress, $13.95
The Shyness and Social Anxiety Workbook, $15.95
The Anger Control Workbook, $17.95
Family Guide to Emotional Wellness, $24.95
Undefended Love, $13.95
The Great Big Book of Hope, $15.95
Don't Leave it to Chance, $13.95
Emotional Claustrophobia, $12.95
The Relaxation & Stress Reduction Workbook, Fifth Edition, $19.95
The Loneliness Workbook, $14.95
Thriving with Your Autoimmune Disorder, $16.95
Illness and the Art of Creative Self-Expression, $13.95
The Interstitial Cystitis Survival Guide, $14.95
Outbreak Alert, $15.95
Don't Let Your Mind Stunt Your Growth, $10.95
Energy Tapping, $14.95
Under Her Wing, $13.95
Self-Esteem, Third Edition, $15.95
Women's Sexualitites, $15.95
Knee Pain, $14.95
Helping Your Anxious Child, $12.95
Breaking the Bonds of Irritable Bowel Syndrome, $14.95
Multiple Chemical Sensitivity: A Survival Guide, $16.95
Dancing Naked, $14.95
Why Are We Still Fighting, $15.95
From Sabotage to Success, $14.95
Parkinson's Disease and the Art of Moving, $15.95
A Survivor's Guide to Breast Cancer, $13.95
Men, Women, and Prostate Cancer, $15.95
Make Every Session Count: Getting the Most Out of Your Brief Therapy, $10.95
Virtual Addiction, $12.95
After the Breakup, $13.95
Why Can't I Be the Parent I Want to Be?, $12.95
The Secret Message of Shame, $13.95
The OCD Workbook, $18.95
Tapping Your Inner Strength, $13.95
Binge No More, $14.95
When to Forgive, $12.95
Practical Dreaming, $12.95
Healthy Baby, Toxic World, $15.95
Making Hope Happen, $14.95
I'll Take Care of You, $12.95
Survivor Guilt, $14.95
Children Changed by Trauma, $13.95
Understanding Your Child's Sexual Behavior, $12.95
The Self-Esteem Companion, $10.95
The Gay and Lesbian Self-Esteem Book, $13.95
Making the Big Move, $13.95
How to Survive and Thrive in an Empty Nest, $13.95
Living Well with a Hidden Disability, $15.95
Overcoming Repetitive Motion Injuries the Rossiter Way, $15.95
What to Tell the Kids About Your Divorce, $13.95
The Divorce Book, Second Edition, $15.95
Claiming Your Creative Self: True Stories from the Everyday Lives of Women, $15.95
Taking Control of TMJ, $13.95
What You Need to Know About Alzheimer's, $15.95
Winning Against Relapse: A Workbook of Action Plans for Recurring Health and Emotional Problems, $14.95

Call **toll free, 1-800-748-6273**, or log on to our online bookstore at **www.newharbinger.com** to order. Have your Visa or Mastercard number ready. Or send a check for the titles you want to New Harbinger Publications, Inc., 5674 Shattuck Ave., Oakland, CA 94609. Include $4.50 for the first book and 75¢ for each additional book, to cover shipping and handling. (California residents please include appropriate sales tax.) Allow two to five weeks for delivery.

Prices subject to change without notice.